All Our Languages

A Handbook for the Multilingual Classroom

David Houlton

Edward Arnold

REV:01-18 EXP:19-99 AB SIZ: 9.02

First published 1985
by Edward Arnold (Publishers) Ltd
41 Bedford Square, London WC1B 3DQ

Reprinted 1988

British Library Cataloguing in Publication Data

ISBN 0 7131 7312 2

Set in Linoterm Univers by The Castlefield Press, Moulton, Northampton.
Printed in Great Britain by
Thomson Litho Ltd, East Kilbride, Scotland

About this book

This is the second of two books, published by the Schools Council Mother Tongue Project[1], which are concerned with the needs of the multilingual primary classroom.

The first, *Supporting Children's Bilingualism*[2], examines some of the policy issues that primary schools and LEAs will need to discuss when considering the type of resources and in-service support needed by teachers who wish to take account of their pupils' diverse language experiences.

The present book focuses more closely on classroom practice. It addresses itself to the teacher who, having accepted the arguments for recognising children's mother tongue skills, asks the question — how do I get started? And, once started — where do I go from here?

In the book we report on the thinking and practice of teachers, from a wide variety of multilingual primary schools, who co-operated with the Schools Council Mother Tongue Project to develop their own responses to the languages of their pupils.

The main sections of the book record some of the initiatives which these teachers have taken; the approaches they have found successful; the kind of materials they have used; the ways in which they have worked with parents and local communities; and their collaboration with bilingual colleagues.

We hope that the accounts of their classroom activities will be of interest to other teachers with multilingual classes, those who are looking for starting points for introducing language diversity into the curriculum, as well as those who want to extend work that is already under way.

Contents

Acknowledgements

This book is the outcome of more than two years' work by one of the largest writing teams imaginable, so it would be impossible to mention by name everybody who has made a contribution. But to those I omit, my thanks are no less sincere.

First, I should like to thank those colleagues from different LEAs who took on a key role in supporting local groups of teachers during the development and trial periods of the book and offering me advice on how best to present the material that they provided. They are: Audrey Gregory, Otto Polling, and Norah Woollard (Berkshire); Kuldip Singh Rai (Birmingham); Jane Bingham and Akram Khan-Cheema (Bradford); Anne Hall and Malcolm Peckham (Buckinghamshire); Ted Jackson (Cleveland); David Pritchard (Coventry); Maggie Halsey and Marie Quinn (Hertfordshire); Ann-Marie Davies (ILEA); Norman Bonnett, Anita Henderson and Maggie Vigor (Kirklees); Janet Knight, Kath Martin and Brian Turner (Lancashire); Lakhpat Rai and Ian Witham (Leeds); Rena Cervi and Roger Wheeler (Leicestershire); Jenny Andrea (Manchester); Mary McKenna (Merton); Rita Beaumont (Newham); Ann Fox, Rashida Spencer and Jenny Vale (Northamptonshire); Jim Chandley and Shukla Kumar (Nottinghamshire); Maggie Buckley, Carole Cressey and Hugh Kelly (Oldham); Tony Kerr (Sheffield); Dorothy Barraclough and Jean Eckersley (Wakefield); Tricia Patterson (Walsall), and Elaine Brittan (Waltham Forest).

Over a hundred and fifty teachers have been involved with this book, either through supplying case studies of classroom practice or by providing feedback on particular chapters. And beyond them are the countless children who made the whole exercise possible and worthwhile. My thanks go to all of them.

We are grateful to the following people for their help in supplying photographs for this book: Roger Bradley, Cathy Ball and Delia Hemmings. The cover photograph was provided by Peter Handford, with assistance from Audrey Gregory and the children of Katesgrove School, Reading.

I wish to thank my colleagues at the former Schools Council, Helen Carter, Director of Programme Four; Alma Craft, Co-ordinator for Multicultural Education; and Deborah Manley, the project's Editor, who offered invaluable advice at every stage in the proceedings. Thanks are due also to Richard Willey who so ably assisted with the early draft of the book, my colleagues Hasina Nowaz and Maria Roussou, and to Paula Tansley, the project's Evaluator, who should take much of the credit for the quality of the feedback we received from teachers during the book's trial stage.

Thanks go to Josephine Heiman and Lyn Keen who did an excellent job in typing the manuscripts. Finally I wish to acknowledge the financial support received from the Commission of the European Communities, without which this work would not have been possible.

David Houlton

We have introduced some Panjabi and Gujarati mother tongue teaching in our school . . . The next step is for class teachers who are not bilingual to discuss how they can co-operate with the mother tongue teachers and help give more status to children's mother tongues in the normal classroom curriculum.

I have only a handful of bilingual children in my class. Even so I still want to value their languages. What I need now is guidance on how to go about it in a way that won't alienate other children in the class.

In a school like ours where one community language is in such a large majority it is very easy to forget that there are children in the school who speak other languages such as Turkish, Cantonese, Greek and Arabic. We now need to give a lot more thought to how we can also support these in the classroom.

At the last count we had thirty different languages in the school. With the best will in the world I don't think we could ever provide mother tongue teaching in all of them. But I'm sure we could do much more to recognise the languages in our day-to-day work.

Introduction

Different situations and backgrounds

As the statements on the previous page suggest, teachers will be coming to this book from different teaching situations. Many will be familiar with classrooms where one of the major community languages such as Bengali, Gujarati, Panjabi or Urdu is spoken by a majority of the children. In other cases, it will be more normal to teach classes that include children from a wide range of language groups. Some teachers may be accustomed to schools where English is the main mother tongue and where there are just a few bilingual children in each class. In addition, the teachers themselves will have varied language backgrounds. A large number, for instance, would possibly describe themselves as monolingual English speakers. Some will speak a regional dialect of English or recall having done so in childhood. And there will be others with knowledge of a language other than English including, in some cases, one or more of the languages spoken by children in their classrooms.

All this makes for a diverse group of readers. But we should point out that this is no more heterogeneous than the group of teachers whose classroom initiatives actually form the basis of this book. They too have varied personal backgrounds and professional situations.

Something in common

What all these teachers have in common, however, is that their daily contact with bilingual children has encouraged them to review their responses to the language skills that exist in the multilingual classroom. Working from the basic principle of wishing to build on the language experiences that children bring to school, they have begun to consider just what steps they might adopt. One teacher's question, 'Do you have another language you understand?', brought the following response from an 11-year-old girl:

> *I speak English at school, Gujarati on my way home to my friends. I read books at Mosque in Urdu, and I learn passages from the Koran in Arabic . . . My mum speaks Marathi.*

The teacher's first reaction was one of anxiety. 'How can the child cope? . . . surely she must confuse the different languages?' Yet the child seemed to cope remarkably well. She had no emotional difficulties and her English showed no signs of 'interference' from her other languages.

Slowly the teacher began to conclude that perhaps the child's multilingual experience had provided her with an *insight into language* that was *quite incomprehensible to the monolingual person*. For this teacher here was a starting point from which he could begin to inform himself about his pupils' languages, and consider ways in which they might be given more recognition in the curriculum.

Changing responses

Responding positively to the home languages of ethnic minority children is a very recent development in British schools. Traditionally emphasis was placed almost exclusively on giving the children sufficient command of English to enable them to follow a normal classroom curriculum. In general the mother tongue was thought to have little place in this. Indeed, many schools actively discouraged children from using the mother tongue for fear of impeding progress in English.

Gradually responses have begun to change. As more teachers have become interested in their pupils' home backgrounds, their cultural traditions and their beliefs, they have begun to recognise the central importance of the mother tongue. They have come to see the multicultural curriculum as being also a multilingual one. What is now emerging from the experience of teachers is that according positive recognition to ethnic minority children's mother tongues can have important educational benefits for the bilingual children themselves, as well as for the class as a whole.

An aid to learning

For bilingual children, use of the mother tongue can be an aid to learning English as a second language. Teachers are finding their traditional misgivings that encouragement of the mother tongue might hinder progress in English have not been borne out. Moreover, experience and, increasingly, research[1] indicate that use of the mother tongue can be a positive support to all-round intellectual development, and a significant aid to children's confidence and self-esteem.

Developing confidence and self-esteem

In the words of one teacher who works in a school which over the last few years has been developing initiatives of the sort described in this book:

> *I now find something that was difficult to find when I first worked in the school — children healthily able to 'be' who they feel themselves to be. To talk in their first language if they choose to; to talk about how they speak at home and with whom; where they were born and what they like to eat; not as a novelty, but rather as part of everyday classroom life.*

Encouraging language awareness

Monolingual children can also gain from an accepting attitude to linguistic diversity. Frequently, teachers emphasise that once they have begun to encourage and explore the use of mother tongues other than English it has led naturally into work with all children on different forms of language. Thus the class as a whole, including the teacher, can be given new insights into language and helped towards a more positive view of languages that are beyond their personal experience.

Celebrating cultural diversity

A wider, more general reason for involving all children in learning about linguistic diversity is that this is an integral part of a school's response to our multicultural society; of positively celebrating cultural differences; of valuing the distinctive contributions of children from ethnic minority groups. In this sense support for the mother tongue can be a major element in the school's approach to negating racist attitudes.

Opening up new approaches

Responding to language diversity in the classroom can play an important part in opening up new methods of working with bilingual colleagues, local communities and parents, as well as with one's own pupils. It can help teachers appreciate the value of children working collaboratively in order to share their experiences and learn from each other. And, as one teacher has pointed out, it can provide valuable opportunities for teachers to appreciate their pupils' skills at first hand.

A variety of responses

Much of the thinking about linguistic diversity in schools is still in its early stages. There are relatively few sources to which teachers can turn for advice and there is certainly no single, generally-accepted approach for the classroom. As a result, many teachers are exploring for themselves different ways of acknowledging the linguistic resources that their pupils have to offer. The examples given in the following sections of the book reflect something of the variety of approaches that have been developed.
   We need to stress, however, that these examples of practice and the discussion accompanying them are not intended as a packaged panacea to the needs of the multilingual classroom. They can be looked at in different ways. For instance, as an individual teacher you may find them of interest as a collection of strategies on which to model ideas for your own classroom. Alternatively, with a group of colleagues you may wish to take the examples as a framework within which you can begin to formulate a more cohesive school policy towards linguistic diversity. Either way, we offer the book as a practical guide to those teachers who are working to see the language curriculum of the multicultural primary school reflect more fully the experiences that children themselves are able to contribute.

1 Finding out about children's languages

We are not allowed to speak our own language at school. We can speak French, though, because French is in the school's curriculum . . . I remember thinking when I was younger that maybe, somehow, my language, the language of my parents wasn't a real language[1].

As we begin to consider how we might give more recognition to our pupils' home languages, it is timely for us to be reminded that even primary-age children, like the secondary student quoted above, may feel that their language is not a 'real' one and has no place in school. The process of reversing children's perceptions is a gradual one. But perhaps a first step is for us, as teachers, to know more about out pupils' language repertoires and to have some understanding of the wider linguistic context within which children operate outside school[2].

For the school as a whole information on children's languages is necessary for providing appropriate staffing, for general resource allocation and as a basis for formulating and implementing policies on language in general and on mother tongue support in particular. At a basic level such information can be incorporated into normal school records. Pupils' mother tongues can be recorded, for example, as part of the information required when children first arrive in school. More detailed information on ways in which children use their mother tongues, and on the extent to which their range of language skills is maintained and developed as they grow up, can be incorporated into on-going reading and language development records.

Much of the process of investigating children's languages may take place in less formalised ways. Class teachers can find out naturally about their pupils' language experiences through their normal work with children, for example through classroom discussion and through contacts with parents and communities. Two general points have emerged from discussion with teachers. First, teachers who have become involved in exploring the linguistic diversity present in their classrooms often comment that the work has proved to have considerable benefits not only for those children who spoke more than one language, but for the class as a whole, including the teacher. At the same time as the conceptual development and sense of self of the bilingual child were being supported, all children could be given new perceptions of language variety. Finding out about the particular skills which children bring with them to school can thus lead into more widely based classwork on language, involving all children.

A second aspect often emphasised by teachers is the importance of close consultation with parents over conducting investigations into mother tongues. If enquiries within the school are to be pursued in the atmosphere of openness and confidence which is essential for productive results, parents need to be closely involved in the approaches which teachers develop. This is important not only because parents can provide invaluable help to teachers but also because some parents may have an overriding concern that their children learn English and may not at once understand the school's interest in their mother tongue.

Involving all children

One way of helping to make investigation of language relevant to the class as a whole is to enquire about dialects as well as languages[3]. Many teachers now feel that speakers of community languages should not be divided off and questioned separately. All children in the class can be asked about the languages they speak and the differences which emerge can then be examined and discussed. The advantage of this type of approach is that it is non-exclusive and all children become involved from the start in finding out about linguistic diversity.

With junior-age children questions like those below could be used as starting points for discussion. Teachers of younger children may wish to prepare their own modified versions:

> Do you speak a language other than English?
> In what part of the world is this language spoken?
> How well can you speak this language?
>   (a bit/quite well/very well)
> Can you read and write this language?
> How much (and when) do you use this language?
> Which dialects of English do you speak?
> What part of the world, or what part of Britain, is this dialect mainly
>   spoken in?
> How much and when do you use this dialect?
> Which languages or dialects would you most like to learn if you had
>   the chance?

Using a questionnaire[4]

A group of teachers in one authority extended these questions to probe in more detail when and with whom children used languages other than English. They devised a questionnaire which explored the language of communication with different members of the immediate and extended

5

family, as well as with friends and acquaintances. It also asked questions about the language used in various social situations such as playtime, shopping or the classroom, for example:

> I usually speak to my mother in _____
>
> My brother usually speaks to me in _____
>
> I usually speak to my grandfather in_____
>
> When I play games I usually speak in_____
>
> While I am watching TV I usually speak in _____

Other questions were about the language of thoughts or of dreams, such as:

> When I talk to myself inside my head in a maths lesson, I usually talk in
>
> _____
>
> The people in my dreams usually speak in_____

Literacy and attendance at mother tongue classes were also investigated:

> Can you read the language you speak at home?_____
>
> Do you go to classes after school, or at the weekend?_____
>
> If YES, what language(s) do you learn there? _____
>
> _____

A learning experience

The teachers' experiences in drafting and using this questionnaire raise a number of general points which may be relevant to other teachers wanting to find out more about their pupils' languages.

In addition to providing information about the children, and opening up the question of appropriate educational response to bilingual pupils, the process of the enquiry became a productive learning experience for the teachers[5]. The teachers involved found that the investigation provided insights into children's use of language in different situations, and also into the range of languages, other than English, used by their pupils. But even more important than the statistical information and general conclusions was the interest engendered among teachers and children in the range of language experiences that exist in the classroom.

When drafting their questionnaire the teachers had been worried that children might not be able to cope with some of the questions, such as 'What language do you think in?'. But they found that they had underestimated the children's ability and receptiveness. In practice the children had used their own phraseology to establish what was meant and almost all were able to comprehend the questions. Many children in fact elaborated their answers and provided considerable supplementary information. The teachers concluded that, given genuine interest and support, children are often pleased to display and share their abilities and knowledge about languages.

The teachers involved chose to ask the questions in a variety of ways. Most held one-to-one interviews with the children; in some cases the teacher recorded responses and in others each child wrote the answers. Some teachers favoured giving the questionnaire to the class as a whole with the children recording a simple written response, so that information could be gathered from a large number of children in a relatively short time.

At the start a number of the teachers involved with the questionnaire were tentative about investigating their pupils' mother tongues because of the severe limitations of their own knowledge:

> How can we with our almost embarrassing lack of knowledge about something so vital to the child, assess the level of mother tongue operation in any situation?

But despite such misgivings all the teachers found that in practice once they had begun finding out about the children's languages it became a stimulating and instructive process for themselves and for their pupils. Bilingual children gained self-confidence by being able to display what they knew, and the languages they could speak were discussed with interest by the class as a whole.

New insights

Teachers who have conducted investigations of this sort often find that they can promote new insights into the abilities and educational experiences of their pupils, so much so that radical reappraisals are often necessary. In some cases children whom teachers have considered to have learning difficulties are found to be capable of operating in two or three languages:

> My mother tongue is Kutchi. My first language is Kutchi. My second language was Chage. My third language was English. I learnt my first language with my family. I learnt my second language by saying ABC. I was not able to pronounce but I tried my best to keep it up. Then I got used to it. I learnt my third language by ABC in school. It was different from the other languages. I tried my best to keep it up, but I was not able to say . . . it. Then I learnt by saying some words . . . from that time I know how to speak the language.

Extending knowledge

This can sometimes lead teachers into unknown areas:

> What is Chage?
> How many people speak it?
> Where is it mainly used?
> Has it a written vocabulary and literature?

As you begin to investigate your own pupils' languages you are likely to find that similar questions arise. In trying to answer them you could begin by approaching the children themselves or their parents, some of whom may prove a valuable source of information. To supplement what you learn in this way you might wish to consult a reference book. Unfortunately there is a shortage of publications that provide the sort of succinct information you would be seeking. But we have found Kenneth Katzner's Languages of the World helpful[6], a copy of which would be a useful addition to your staffroom library.

Other approaches

Another possible approach to finding out about children's languages is to develop language as a topic or theme. For example, a 'languages board' can be set up to which all children, including the very young, may contribute. They may be asked if they can identify different scripts, whether they can write them, where they have seen them, etc. You might suggest they bring examples of different languages from home, and parents can be encouraged to contribute.

In one school, where the children are aged between 5 and 11, the centrepiece for a languages board was a map of the world, labelled with questions about families' countries of origin and the languages spoken there as well as at home in Britain. Accompanying the map was a bar chart, prepared by the children, showing the languages of the school. Again, questions were displayed in order to encourage the children to examine the findings and extract further information for themselves. The teacher responsible says:

> . . . *Those children who could write in their languages were asked to provide examples of their scripts. Others brought in books, stamps, magazines, newspapers, foodwrappers, etc. written in their own and other languages. These were all displayed and provided interesting talking points.*

To illustrate the benefits for the children, she describes one child's reaction:

> *One child, from Ghana, who would never discuss her language before, has now produced a sample of script in Twi and is generally far more willing to participate in activities of this sort.*

In another school the centrepiece was a display, researched by the children themselves, showing words and symbols for 'peace' in different languages and cultures.

Teachers who have used the idea of a languages board as a starting point would stress its two-fold value. First, the actual process of gathering material and information for the board is in itself worthwhile since it encourages the children to become more aware of languages in their lives and to share their knowledge with others. Second, it helps to create a climate in school where the children know it is legitimate to discuss their diverse language experiences, an important pre-requisite for any investigation by teachers into their pupils' use of language.

Children as investigators

This principle of involving children actively in gathering information on the languages of the school or classroom is one that many teachers would favour. Some have incorporated it into mathematics activities as a basis for compiling histograms, Venn diagrams or pie charts. For example, in a small class of 7-year-olds, the children investigated each others' home languages and discovered that:

> *One child spoke Urdu, five Panjabi, four Gujarati, two Bengali and one Cantonese. This information was then used in a maths lesson to make a block graph. Different colours were used for each language and English was included as the teacher's language. The children counted the numbers in their mother tongues. A large chart headed* These are our languages *was then made . . . children's names and languages were displayed alongside the graph so it was clear which language each child spoke.*

A class of 5- and 6-year-olds presented their findings as shown below.

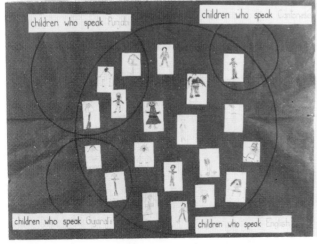

Other teachers have encouraged children to write about, or discuss in groups, the languages that they see, hear or use.

When I am coming home from School, I hear people talking in one of the indian Languages. I went to Spain a long time ago, and I heard someone talking in Spanish. I have got a spanish pen-friend in Spain called Marie. My Auntie and Uncle live in Birmingham, and they speak in Birmingham English. My Grandfather lives in Liverpool, and he speaks Liverpool English. I have got a sister, who is married, and can speak Irish and English. My dad can speak Irish as well.

I can speak Welsh. I like speaking in Welsh. this is how to count to twenty . . . . un, dia, tre, pedwer, pimp, llwerdn, sith, uwith, now, deg, indeg, indegdia, indeg, tre, indegpedwer, indegpimp undegnow, diateg,. It is easy to read Welsh but not that easy to say it. I can speak English as well, Wesh in Wales is cymraeg

Languages that I speak

I speak gujarati. I can speak gujarati very well because I speak gujarati to My my mum, dad, and my two sisters. I can write a bit of gujarati. Well I go to a special school on sundays. I have just started about a month ago. I can read gujarati quite well but I am still learning. My mum can speak other languages like punjabi. So can my dad. I can count in my language but I can only count upto 5 and I am going to write it in my language એક્ક

એલ

ન ત્રણ

ચાર

પાંચ.

In the example below a teacher is discussing patterns of language use with a group of 7- and 8-year-olds. In the group are Devinder, Fatema, Khyati and Rajan:

Teacher   *Which languages do you use when you speak to people in your family? . . .*

Devinder   *I speak to my Grandma in Panjabi. She doesn't speak English so I always speak to her in Panjabi.*

Teacher   *(to Khyati) What language do you use to speak to your Grandma?*

Khyati   *Sometimes I use English and sometimes I use Gujarati.*

Teacher   *Both?*

Khyati   *Yes, but mostly Gujarati.*

Rajan   *Miss, Rafiq's dad can't speak English.*

Teacher   *What language does he speak?*

Fatema   *He speaks Kutchi . . . Miss, my family can speak Kutchi, English . . . and Urdu . . . and Gujarati.*

Teacher   *Do you understand Panjabi?*

Fatema   *No . . . I understand a little bit because some of the words are like Urdu.*

Even a short discussion like this can highlight some interesting information. The children seem to have no difficulty giving the correct names of their languages. They are aware of their own bilingual abilities and that certain family relationships require them to use a particular language. They are also aware of the languages spoken by others. Fatema, for instance, knows that Rafiq's dad speaks Kutchi and that her own family has a wide language repertoire. She is even able to detect similarities between languages.

A further approach would be to devise a practical research activity that could assist children in charting their personal patterns of language use, for example, drawing a flow chart to show which members of your family speak and understand which languages.[7]

At first, you may feel that an activity like this is most appropriate for bilingual children since it is they who will probably need to display most linguistic variety in their dealings with family members. This is not our experience, since we have found that many apparently monolingual children live in families where other languages are used from time to time. And once the activity is extended beyond charting the patterns of language use, to include the pet names and terms of endearment that appear in all families, you immediately begin to enter the diverse world of dialects and even private languages, all of which are part of many pupils' repertoires. Indeed, when you begin to explore children's experience of dialects, many further opportunities are likely to present themselves. For example, a class of 10- and 11-year-olds decided to survey, with the help of a questionnaire, their parents' language experiences. Their teacher writes:

> . . . *we found parents who could read, write or speak French, German, Welsh, Irish, Jamaican Creole, Panjabi, Arabic, Urdu and, very interestingly, Urdu shorthand. We also had several examples of secret languages and codes from parents, as well as some slang from World War II.*

Care and sensitivity

However, this same teacher recognises in a salutary way that, while any of the strategies we have described could be successful, it is vital that investigation of children's languages be conducted with care and sensitivity:

> *One boy has so far shown disdain . . . his father is a senior figure of the local Urdu-speaking community and has said he wants nothing to do with it all. A girl says she's afraid of being laughed at by me and the other children if she says anything in Urdu. Of the two West Indian girls one has parents born in Barbados and insists they never speak anything but standard English. The other has parents of Jamaican origin who speak 'patois' but at the moment she is very reticent about it . . . Perhaps they think we are meddling in their private affairs.*

In reminding us of these dangers the teacher is also highlighting a recurring theme throughout the chapters that follow: in order for children to be able to share their language skills with others, they need to feel that the classroom atmosphere is hospitable to diversity and that differences can be discussed openly and with mutual trust. Such an atmosphere is likely to take some time to develop, but an important ingredient in creating it is to ensure that whenever possible the language and cultural activities you encourage are not restricted to bilingual pupils. Ample opportunity should be provided for participation from all members of the class.

2 Language diversity across the curriculum

> *Whilst all staff in the school agree that we want our children to feel positive about the variety of languages in our community, there is by no means a consensus about how this might be approached.*

This teacher's words probably reflect the situation of many other colleagues in multilingual schools where at present there is no overall policy relating to language diversity, nor even any broad agreement on the classroom strategies that have been found to be effective.

Without wishing to deny the importance of a whole-school policy in response to language, experience has shown that even where no policy exists, there is a great deal that individual teachers can accomplish. Indeed, in the school mentioned above class teachers have done much towards encouraging their pupils to talk confidently about their language skills, to share their experiences with others and, gradually, to have an increased awareness of the many forms of language that exist around them.

A multilingual atmosphere

What these and other teachers would stress, however, is that language diversity is not something to be confined to a single subject on the curriculum or a particular group of children. Rather, they have found that it can permeate the atmosphere of the classroom and their approach to all their pupils. In order to outline some ways of translating this principle into practice, we'll begin by focusing on a compilation of approaches prepared by teachers in one authority, based on the work that they and their colleagues have undertaken in their own classrooms.

A chart — some starting points

Their ideas are condensed into the following chart, designed to give an overview of how some of the major areas of the primary curriculum might begin to draw upon the language resources of pupils and their families.

LANGUAGE DIVERSITY ACROSS THE CURRICULUM
— some starting points

Names and naming systems
* Look at the names of the children in the class. What do they mean?
* Encourage bilingual children to write their names in their home language. Monolingual pupils could learn to write their names in a different script.
* Discuss naming traditions in different cultures. For instance in Indonesia a child is sometimes not given a name until the age of 8. The name is then chosen to fit the personality.
* Discuss name changing practices, e.g., whether different cultures expect women to change their names on marriage. What would the children like to do?
* Why have some famous people chosen to change their names? e.g., Cliff Richard was Harry Webb.

Displaying languages
* Display names for numbers and colours in different languages and scripts. Use these in discussion with children.
* Make books about numbers, colours, visits, cooking activities, visitors, days of the week, months of the year. Use the languages of the classroom to show the scripts, their formation, directionality etc.
* Put up labels in the classroom reflecting children's languages.

Writing and number systems
* Starting with cave paintings you could move on to look at Egyptian hieroglyphics, Phoenician and Greek alphabets. Look at how other scripts and languages have developed from these and how others are even more different (e.g., Chinese, Arabic etc.).
* Examples of different scripts and languages can be examined for their similarities.
* This can be related to maths activities with the languages being classified, using Venn diagrams, according to which alphabet they use — Roman, Greek, Cyrillic, Arabic etc.
* Let the children practise counting and measuring in different languages.
* Introduce the children to picture languages. Try writing English in this way.
* This could lead on to examining other communication systems (e.g., codes, Braille, semaphore, morse, Romany signs, Cherokee).

Cookery
* Talk with the children about their favourite meals.
* Ask them to bring in recipes and invite parents to help.
* Take the children shopping for the ingredients.
* Discuss the names and correct pronunciation of ingredients.
* Many primary children are quite experienced cooks. Let them demonstrate their skills.
* Get the children to describe the activity in pictures and writing. Mount a display with captions in English and other languages.

Songs, poems and rhymes

* Older pupils, brothers and sisters can be a valuable resource for teaching the teacher and children songs and rhymes in their own language.
* Parents can also be very useful.
* 'Space Poem 1: from Lanka to Gagarin' by Edwin Morgan. This can be enjoyed purely for its sounds, but it can also be looked at to see why those sounds (derived from Russian words) are particularly effective and suitable for the subject. Pupils could try making up their own sound poems using sounds from their home languages as well as English.
* Reading and listening to poems and stories in different dialects and accents can encourage pupils to find out about the varieties of language at home and in the neighbourhood. Make tape recordings and transcripts of these.

Accents and dialects

* Discussion of accents and dialects can be a regular feature of classroom activity. But it needs to be approached sensitively. Don't use pupils' accents to begin with. Use famous people or friends on tape. Put this into a realistic context like making up a play.
* Look at how difficult it is to convey accents in writing.
* Talk about accents in different countries and how most countries have regional varieties.
* Look at how people use accents in different situations.

Topic work

* Many classroom topics can lend themselves to learning about language and languages. For example, topics on 'Ourselves', 'Food', 'The neighbourhood', 'Celebrations', 'Weddings' have encouraged children to share their language experiences and become more aware of languages around them.
* Other topics such as 'Communication', 'History of writing', 'Languages around the world' can focus in more depth on language diversity.
  With a topic on 'Comics and newspapers' you could:
* Make a collection of comics and newspapers written in other languages as well as English.
* Analyse their contents, looking at how speech is represented, headlines used, choice of pictures etc. Look in more depth for racist, sexist or political bias.
* Carry out a similar exercise involving newspapers in English and other languages. Parents could become involved with this.
* Make your own comic or newspaper using the languages of the school, the class and the community.

Games

* Children are likely to be familiar with games in different languages and dialects.
* Get them to teach each other games that they know, using the appropriate language or dialect.
* This could be followed by making a book — 'Games we know' or 'Games from around the world'.

Individual readers will, no doubt, have their own thoughts on how to make use of it. But the teachers whose work is reflected in the chart offer the following advice by way of introduction.

Using the chart

* These ideas are starting points for teachers who want to foster their pupils' interest and knowledge of language, in its broadest sense.
* They are based on the premise that teachers and schools use teaching methods based on generally accepted good practice — child-centred, collaborative learning, a classroom atmosphere conducive to the free exchange of information and ideas between pupil and pupil, and pupils and teachers, and a close involvement between the school and community.
* Language is a very personal, sensitive area of the curriculum, and a lot of the ideas suggested can be used as and when a suitable moment appears, especially with very young children.
* Most of these ideas are not meant to be used as a basis for a lesson on language, but as part of a much broader-based topic, where language plays an incidental or more major part.
* Where possible we have given an idea of when the activity could be used, or how a topic could be developed using the expertise of the bilingual pupils, parents, or teachers in the school.
* Of necessity, the ideas are not fully developed, and only touch on the range of possibilities open to teachers. It is up to you to adapt, use and extend them to suit yourself and your pupils.
* Great sensitivity will be needed in many schools where there isn't already a positive attitude to linguistic diversity and our multicultural society. However, those teachers who are already trying to incorporate anti-racist teaching strategies into their work will, we hope, find some of these activities useful in that area.

Further activities

In the rest of this chapter, we'll expand upon the ideas shown in the chart by drawing upon more detailed examples of classroom initiatives undertaken by primary teachers from a variety of multilingual schools in other areas of the country. For convenience, we'll keep to the curriculum areas mentioned in the chart, although this means there are inevitably some overlaps.

Topic work

Topic work occupies such a central position in the primary curriculum that for many teachers, it has been the most obvious starting point for exploring their pupils' language experiences. For some teachers the approach has been consciously to select themes that conveniently lend themselves to the inclusion of multilingual elements[1]. Some examples of these are found in the chart.

Other teachers have preferred to explore language diversity as part of a theme which is already under way or planned for the class. In some cases they have displayed considerable ingenuity with topics which would not initially appear to offer a great deal of multilingual potential.

In one school, for example, a topic on 'Birds' was used in this way:

In the lower junior classes language diversity has become an element in topic work, this term on birds. Stories have been the main means of developing language awareness within the theme. A little French book, Printemps, *provided images of the coming spring with the appearance of the swallow. Clear strong shapes in the illustrations were used in painting and cut-out silhouettes.* Ma Sparrow's Babies *in English and Bengali has a chorus which is repeated throughout the cumulative storyline and characters are named in the Bengali words for their occupations.* The Two Cockerels *in English and Yoruba proved a source of interest. Most children were amazed to learn that Yoruba is just one of many, many African languages, and were intrigued that they could identify the meaning of a few Yoruba words with the help of the parallel English text.*

Tracing migratory patterns of birds brought opportunities to identify language areas, to talk about the geographical 'continuum' of language communities and briefly, to relate bird migration to the migrations of people within and between countries and the resultant 'borrowing' among languages.

Before launching any topic with your class you would normally expect to plan how it might be extended beyond the initial starting point. If you have not been in the habit of building a multilingual element into your work you will almost certainly want to plan the topic in some detail. To help with this, the following chart shows how a popular theme, 'harvest', can take on a multilingual (and multicultural) character. The chart itself was prepared by a group of teachers as part of an in-service training course. Notice how they have tried to ensure a balance between all the normal primary school activities whilst providing opportunities for all children to contribute their own experiences and concurrently share in the languages and cultures of others.

HARVEST
an example of a recurring school theme which can enable recognition of linguistic and cultural diversity

The school library
1 Tape recordings of 'harvest stories' in different languages.
2 Class books on display, including cookery books.
3 Displays of food.
4 Pictures of harvests from a wide variety of countries.
5 A good book selection on harvest themes from all over the world.
6 Finding out tasks displayed in library.

Display work, signs and posters
1 Use of photographs to depict harvest produce.
2 Harvest displays in different languages, perhaps some translations made by older children in the school
3 Fruit and vegetable paintings together with real examples, named in different languages.
4 Food alphabets.

Science
1 Soil.
2 Agricultural methods and crops world-wide.
3 Climate.
4 Nutritional aspects of food in different environments.
5 Cycle — Steiner's rotting apple.
6 Introducing 'own' harvest — growing of alfalfa/mustard/ sunflower seeds.
7 Seed dispersal.
8 Soil/water experiments.
9 Progression of growth from a seed to the kitchen shelf.
10 Food labels as a starting point for finding out about food from different countries.
11 Collection of harvest fruits and nuts.
12 Planting bulbs.
13 Different types of food storage world-wide.

Games
1 Oranges and lemons.
2 Co-operative version of 'Hot Potato'.
3 A 'Feely-Box'.
4 Dingle-Dangle.
5 Oats and beans.
6 Cumulative shopping games.
7 Apple bobbing.
8 Finger games.
9 Games of different cultural origins evolved from harvest celebrations.
10 Guessing games.
11 Conkers.

Maths activities

1 Symmetry and shape of fruit and vegetables.
2 Fractions.
3 Graphs of different food consumption patterns.
4 Sorting — leading to matrices.
5 Counting of fruits and seeds in different languages.

Cookery

1 Visit a mill.
2 Use flour to make breads of different cultural origins; chapattis, bread, pizza, buckwheat pancakes, etc.
3 Visit the market.
4 Visit an allotment.
5 Use of vegetables, fruits, nuts, fish and staples to cook dishes of a variety of cultural origins.
6 Involvement of parents with cooking of different dishes.
7 Taking a series of photos in the sequence of cooking one item and then making into a dual text book.

Writing

1 Develop the value of sharing through a class book — extend into poetry and 'harvest theme' books.
2 Translate class books into different languages and make transliterations.
3 Make use of examples of packaging and advertising.
4 Make use of food labels in different languages.

Music-making

1 Instrument-making using gourds and dried seeds.
2 Harvest songs and dances from different cultural traditions, e.g., Panjabi harvesting songs and dances from the Indian sub-continent.
3 Thanksgiving songs generally.
4 Sharing songs.
5 Creating music to simulate weather, farm machinery, animals, etc.
6 Creating music to accompany harvest stories.
7 The use of related themes through movement.

Art and craft

1 Vegetable printing.
2 Natural dyeing/batik.
3 Collage using seeds.
4 Corn dollies and harvest craft traditions in other countries.
5 Colours, named in different languages.

Writing and number systems

It is often valuable to introduce children to the writing and number systems associated with the languages of the classroom or community[2]. At a very simple level, children of all ages in the primary school enjoy seeing different number symbols, learning to form the numerals themselves, and playing counting games based on them.

I introduced counting in different languages. Counting-cards and hand shapes with numbers up to ten in different languages and scripts were displayed and frequently referred to while following the regular maths scheme. Counting and number-based games were played in different languages and the children became quite adept at counting in Swahili, Panjabi, French, Russian and Spanish.

You may prefer to introduce the activity more gradually, as this teacher did with her class of 7–9-year-olds:

We had been working on topics about North American Indians and, later, Romans. Both of these had involved work on signs and symbols . . . We looked at Indian sign language and picture writing, then at Roman letters and numerals. We went on to collect numbers, in symbols and words, in other languages. Help in pronouncing them came from parents and children. We used the numbers in counting games, rhymes and simple sums. The languages included Greek, Gujarati, Hindi, Italian, Maltese, Serbo Croat and Urdu. Our follow-up activities included art work in which bilingual children helped others to write or paint their names and numerals in other languages.

Another teacher describes how this idea could be extended further so as to provide bilingual children with reinforcement in their mother tongue number skills, as well as offering the monolingual children in the class an opportunity to learn about other systems of counting.

The largest group of bilingual children in my class of 7–9-year-olds are Gujarati. There are seven of them.

One day I decided to ask a mum if she could listen to the children counting in Gujarati. She listened to each of the seven children and remarked that they knew the numbers 1 to 10 only. None of the children was able to write them down or read the numbers as figures or in words. I decided it would be a good starting point for embarking on some number work both in English and Gujarati.

I hoped to help the Gujarati- and English-speaking children to record their number work in Gujarati. To this end I enlisted the help of adults who could write Gujarati. We produced worksheets and Hundred Squares in English and Gujarati, and these were later duplicated.

Prior to the children starting these worksheets, many sessions were spent on practical work. We counted objects, we put out hoops and into them put sets of various objects. We listened to a tape recording of a Gujarati speaker counting slowly. Booklets of worksheets were made consisting of activities on the numbers 1 to 10.

The children took their booklets home. The reaction from parents was very encouraging. Several parents came into school with the children and were very pleased with the interest being shown in their mother tongue. One parent gave me a lesson on the Gujarati booklet, going through it page by page.

The interaction among the children during these counting sessions was very interesting. The English speakers were being tested, informally of course, by the Gujarati speakers. One

*enthusiastic Gujarati boy called delightedly, 'Stephen can count
real good from 1 to 12 in Gujarati'. Stephen went home and next
morning came up to me and confidently said, 'I counted up to 12
to my Mum in Gujarati and she said 'That's great!'. Many
English-speaking children asked if they could try writing
Gujarati numbers. Several copied out a Hundred Square.*

*So far, the signs have been encouraging both from children
and parents. There has not been any adverse reaction. In some
ways the children seem to be closer in their relationship with one
another. When working on their Gujarati counting worksheets
and during oral/practical lessons there seemed to be a relaxed
atmosphere as if some unseen barrier had been broken down
within the classroom.*

With older juniors these number activities may be equally applicable. It
is possible, however, that the teacher may also wish to incorporate a
multilingual approach into a mathematically-based topic.

Our fourth example demonstrates this idea at work. Here, a teacher
reports on a measurement topic. She describes how it began by focusing
on the main classroom language, apart from English. But she goes on to
explain how it eventually expanded to include the languages of all the
bilingual pupils.

Throughout her account it is clear just how strong an appeal language
diversity came to have for the class as a whole.

*At the start I decided to enlist outside help. Nothing worked as
well as the personal approach. Two of my ex-pupils were
enthusiastic and offered their services, which proved a great help
to me. They provided me with lists of mathematical terms in
Gujarati. Such words as handspan, cubit, reach, stride, length,
width, etc. It was these same ex-pupils who actually went home,
talked to their parents and asked them if they would be able to
help me and my class in any way. From these enquiries three
parents came to see me. After discussing the type of thing I
wanted to do, they agreed to give up some of their time to come
into school.*

*I decided from the start that I wanted to do the work with the
entire class, rather than isolate the Gujarati speakers. On
reflection, I'm glad I did this. Often I find it is the teacher who is
afraid of the way in which children will react to anything new and
these fears are passed on to the pupils. Anxieties are then aroused
which were sometimes not there in the first place.*

*We began by recapping on general measurement terms. Whilst
we discussed the English terminology I decided to introduce
some of the Gujarati terms for measuring. The children
continued their practical work, but now using both English and*

Gujarati. For example, when the children measured the length and width of the classroom in strides they talked about the Gujarati term for 'stride' which was 'pergla'.

I wrote the Gujarati symbols for these terms on the blackboard alongside the English phonetic spelling. I asked the Gujarati speakers in my class if I was pronouncing the terms correctly. When the children realised I was asking them for help they were only too willing to offer advice. This attitude carried on throughout the entire project. The children had a great deal of fun listening to me and each other making mistakes over pronunciation. The Gujarati-speaking children obviously felt a sense of pride, because they knew how to pronounce the words properly and the other children and I looked to them for help and advice.

The first time I wrote a Gujarati word on the board I ruled a line and wrote the symbols sitting on the line. Immediately the Gujarati speakers put me right. They informed me that the symbols should hang from the line and not sit on it. I asked some of them to show me on the board. All the children in the class attempted to pronounce the Gujarati words and no one seemed particularly embarrassed if they made a mistake. Some of the children said they wished they could hear their own attempts at pronunciation; therefore the idea of the tape recorder was introduced. We taped each other speaking Gujarati and tried to make improvements.

During the practical sessions the children were in groups. Each group had at least one Gujarati-speaking child. Each group did some practical measuring in different ways, then they tried to report to other groups exactly what they had done, using both Gujarati and English terms. While the oral work was being done the children also practised writing the Gujarati symbols for the measurement terms. The ones who really mastered this went on to reinforce their work by doing patterns on screen prints using those symbols.

As the work gathered momentum we decided to produce booklets called The Measurement Family including descriptions and pictures for each measurement term we had used. First we compiled together a description and caricature of one of the measurement family. We chose 'cubit'. The character became Mr Cubit Haath, Haath being the phonetic spelling for the Gujarati word. The word cubit made some children think of a cube shape, fat and square. Therefore Mr Cubit Haath became a small, fat, square-shaped personality eating square-shaped food on square-shaped plates.

Mr Cubit Haath

Mr Cubit Haath is rather fat and he

is always getting into trouble. He

always has a smile on his face. His

skin is very light pink and his cheeks

are rosy red. His hair is brown and

curly. He is alway snoozing off in the

middle of a programme. There is something

unusual about Mr Cubit. When he is trying

to steal some oranges and somebody

is coming he turns to an orange colour.

So nobody can see him.

Whenever we talked about the characters we got into the habit of using both the English and Gujarati terms simultaneously. Likewise, next to the pictures the children wrote the name of each character in English and Gujarati.

The work on the booklets continued until each member of the class had produced a description and picture accompanied by the appropriate English and Gujarati for each member of the measurement family. Then they took their booklets home.

I was pleased with the reaction from the parents. Most of them were pleased to see what the children were doing. There were no objections from any of the parents. Two English parents did stop me in the playground to ask why the children had started to learn Gujarati. I explained that it was something the children enjoyed and were interested in, and as we had some children in the class who spoke Gujarati it seemed silly not to make the most of them. The parents agreed about their children's enthusiasm and interest, and one mother confessed to attempting with difficulty to copy some of the Gujarati symbols. One or two of the Gujarati-speaking parents checked the work the children took home and made certain corrections. This gave me the idea for involving the parents in the completion of the booklets.

I asked the class if any of them would like to translate the descriptions they had written into their own mother tongue. Those children (four of them) who were capable of writing some Gujarati attempted the translations on their own. Some of the other Gujarati speakers asked if they could get help from other members of their family. I was more than willing to let this happen.

Many of the English-speaking children wanted their descriptions translated too. Comments such as 'I wish I could speak more than one language' were heard in the classroom. The Gujarati-speaking parents who came into school helped by translating parts of the children's booklets and then the children tried to copy out the translations. The children also asked their peers for help and advice.

The Panjabi-speaking children then asked if they could translate their descriptions into Panjabi. I was delighted with this request. A similar process of home involvement was encouraged. The children seemed to take particular pride in the written form of the mother tongue. I had one child in the class who spoke and wrote Italian. Of course she wanted to translate her booklet into Italian.

Once the translations were completed I approached various parents (Guajarati, Panjabi, Italian) to see if they would be willing to check the children's work, either at home or in school.

As most of the parents had either seen or heard about the booklets the children were working on, they were much more responsive to my call for help. I think the parents realised we were making a genuine effort with the mother tongue work, and therefore felt their help was really needed and would be much appreciated. I would never try to pretend the children's booklets are perfect, or even near perfect, translations into the various languages. Nevertheless, they have proved to be a successful vehicle for capturing the interest and enthusiasm of the children and the involvement of parents and friends. The children are now talking about producing word games using the languages of the classroom. I take this as an encouraging sign for future work we hope to cover.

Cookery

Cookery in the primary school has long been an activity which teachers have used to help children's development of mathematical and scientific concepts. Nowadays, in many multicultural schools, it has the additional value of helping teachers draw upon their pupils' experience of other languages and cultures[3], sometimes with surprising results.

> *. . . a usually quiet group of Bengali and Panjabi speakers sat down, decided what they wanted to make, drew up a list of ingredients and decided who would bring what — all without any help from me.*

Other teachers have seen it as a valuable opportunity to call upon the expertise of parents.

Here a teacher of junior children writes about her weekly bilingual cookery sessions where she works closely with a parent, Mrs Khan.

Every Friday morning is set aside for cooking. We make English and Indian dishes alternate weeks. This is how we work:

If the recipe is an Indian one, Mrs Khan takes the lead. She talks with the children in Gujarati as the dish is made, step by step. The children's responses are also in Gujarati.

If I cannot follow what she has been saying, I ask her to translate it into English for me, then I talk with the children in English, step by step, in the same way. If I have been able to follow, I follow her Gujarati with my English. Thus Gujarati and English are used alternatively throughout the whole process of preparing, cooking and eating.

If the recipe is an English one, I take the lead, speaking with the children in English. Mrs Khan will follow, stage by stage, in Gujarati. Thus again everything we do is discussed in both languages.

We have labelled as many as possible of the ingredients we use in the following way:
* *English name written in Roman script;*
* *Gujarati name written phonetically in Roman script;*
* *Gujarati name written in Gujarati script.*

In due course we intend to add the names in other languages.

Your reasons for introducing a multilingual element into cookery activities and the approach you adopt will vary according to your school circumstances. But we can offer some general advice based on what teachers have reported to us:

* This sort of activity needs careful advance preparation and may last longer than expected.
* Try to involve the whole class. Only a small group may be able to use the cooker and utensils at any one time but it is important for all children to be able to take part and share in the results.
* Avoid the session developing into a demonstration by an adult with little participation by children.
* If parents are to be involved make sure that they give the children opportunity to talk and join in.
* Whenever possible encourage the children to show what they know and to learn from each other.

Displaying languages

You may feel at times that displays which feature the languages of your pupils may amount to little more than tokenism if the children are not literate in the languages and therefore unable to make full use of them. This is not our experience. In fact we have found that a carefully planned display can sometimes promote a lively positive response from children and offer the teacher a valuable starting point from which to explore other aspects of the school's linguistic diversity.

This was the reaction in a first school where previously children had had little opportunity to see their own languages, and those of others, given a place:

I put up a display of the numbers 1-10 in English and Urdu and the names of the different colours in English, Panjabi, Hindi and Urdu. The display was accompanied by the question, 'Do you think there are children in this school who can speak and read more than one language?'. I also explained what the languages were. Both bilingual and monolingual children have shown great interest in the display. Several children have written numbers in Bengali, Urdu and Hindi to add to the display.

Some children have been so intrigued that they have begun asking me simple questions in Urdu to see if I can understand them. Reaction from the pupils has been very positive. Several members of staff have noticed the display and asked me about it.

Other teachers have preferred to incorporate the languages of the classroom into displays arising from topic work, TV programmes or some other centre of interest:

> *As part of a 'harvest' topic my class of younger juniors visited an Asian greengrocer's near the school and bought a varied selection of fruit and vegetables which they were familiar with. Back at school we displayed them in a corridor with labels in Panjabi and Gujarati. They became a popular talking point as children passed and tried to read the labels to each other.*

Displays of clothes, cooking utensils and artefacts from home have sparked off similar interest in other schools. Unfortunately, initiatives like these are sometimes seen as one-off exercises and this can serve to minimise their value and give rise to complaints of tokenism. To avoid this happening in your school you need to be working for a strong multilingual element in all the displays and signs so that the children's languages do not simply appear when the teacher remembers, but are there, in some form, as a constant reminder that it is a multilingual school.

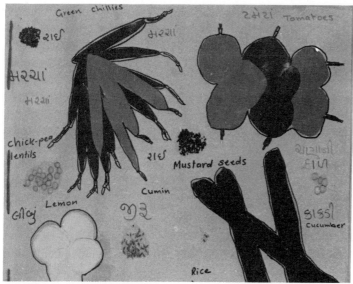

Accents and dialects

In the multilingual classroom linguistic diversity is not confined to the languages of bilingual pupils, although these will certainly provide the main focus for much of your work. The classroom is also likely to include children who speak the local variety of English or who have moved from other areas of Britain bringing their dialects with them. And as the bilingual children interact with their English-speaking peers their own English will soon begin to display some features of local speech. Rather than presenting problems for the teacher all this can help introduce a new language dimension into the work of the class[4].

Some ideas for acknowledging accents and dialects were described in the chart on page 15. Other ideas which teachers have used are:

* carrying out a dialect survey of the school or neighbourhood by interviewing parents, local people, teachers and others who work in the school;
* identifying different dialects and locating them on a map of Britain or the world;
* collecting written and spoken examples of English dialects and making comparisons between them;
* discussing why some dialects have more prestige, or are thought to be more appealing, than others.

With older juniors you might like to consider taking up one teacher's idea of compiling worksheets for use in the classroom. Here is an example completed by a child:

Sheffieldish
How well do you speak Sheffield's very own language?
Translate the following sentences into English:

1 Tweert wateer uns or t'weer in 't wicker.

Where the water run's over the weir in the wicker.

2 Nadenodagooin?

How are you.

3 Thart reight mardy thee.

You are very miserable.

4 Wasup withi?

What is the matter with you.

5 Al nottellthi ageean.

I am not going to tell you again.

6 Shutthigob oral shuttit fothi.

Stop talking or I will stop you with my Fist.

7   Giuzit.

give it to me.

8   Tha wonster wesh thi eeroils aht.

You should listen more carefully.

9   Ayampt eeard nowt.

I have not heard anything.

10   Summats upeer.

Somethings wrong.

Think of three more sentences in Sheffieldish and write them below:

1   *Weers all wateer cumin frum.*

2   *Ee by gum wats apanin.*

3   *Weerz tha think thaz bin.*

Needless to say this was a very enjoyable activity for the class concerned and one in which all children could participate with some, as the example shows, displaying considerable skill. The class went on to compile lists of dialect words such as those for:

food   *grub, nosh.*

money   *bread, munch.*

playing truant   *wagging it, skiving.*

good   *brill, fab.*

clothes   *clobber, kegs.*

the head   *noggin, bonce.*

They experimented with Cockney rhyming slang and collected poems in their own dialect, like those below:

The Coyal Oyl

Weer reet darn in coyal oyl
Weer muck spats ont twinders
Wiv used all our coyal up
And weer reet darn to cinders
If yon baliffs cum they'll neer findus
Cus weer reet down in coyal oyl
Weer muck spats ont twinders.

A neece cuppa tee

Ee a wud like to gith thee a neece cuppa tea
If only thad cum ont reight day
But that munt cum on Monday
Its me weshin day, an am weshin an weshin me
                                    clooers away

Exciting as this work can be, however, you will need to remember that even primary-age children may regard their dialects as being of low status and therefore be as embarrassed about sharing these with the teacher as their bilingual peers are about their own mother tongues. Also, children, like adults, may have strong views about the worth of particular dialects and the people who speak them, and this could be a source of classroom controversy. So we repeat again our earlier advice to handle discussion with care and sensitivity.

Names and naming systems

With infants or younger juniors you would probably approach work in this area by focusing on the children's own names — what they mean, how they are pronounced, nicknames among friends, pet names in the family, etc. and give all the children the opportunity of seeing their names written in scripts other than English.

With the help of a bilingual colleague I made name cards for all the class. We wrote the children's names in English and in Urdu script. The children watched this being done. We displayed the names in the classroom and the children enjoy trying to recognise each other's names in Urdu. Some have now begun writing their names in Urdu.

From this small beginning this class of 5–6-year-olds went on to look at Eid cards and practise writing the names and greetings that appeared in them in Urdu.

If you are working with older children you might prefer to develop a project around a theme, allowing the class to explore specific aspects in some detail. Here is how one teacher, with a class of 10–11-year-olds, went about it:

It was the beginning of the autumn term, I had a new class, and I decided a project on 'names' would be a very good way of getting to know the children better.

I began by taking into school a collection of pictures of famous people and asked the children if they knew their real names. I used the example of Cliff Richard (Harry Webb) to ask the children why people sometimes chose to change their names. The children went on to discuss the names of other well-known people — pop stars, film stars, explorers. As the week went on children brought in their own pictures including Indian film stars and sports personalities from various ethnic groups. Some of the bilingual children tried to help the other members of the class pronounce the names correctly. They attached great importance to this.

The children tried to say and write their own names in as many different ways as possible. Two teachers in the school helped them to translate their names into Panjabi and Gujarati. Children also wrote their names in Egyptian hieroglyphics, code, paint, printing, embroidery and other media.

The whole class was involved. They split into groups of four or five and took it in turns to work on a particular aspect of the topic. Within the groups some children chose to pair up and work as partners. With a mixed-age and mixed-ability class like mine it is important for each child to have a measure of success. The project offered a lot of scope for this whilst at the same time allowing me to introduce a range of languages as well as aspects of children's religious and cultural lives.

A feature of activities that draw upon children's own experience is that the children are often much more confident about contributing to discussions. In this same class, for instance, the project gave rise to a lot of group talk about the names for foodstuffs, clothing, artefacts from home, etc. This was encouraged by a visit from Naseem, an older sister, who spoke to the class about her recent wedding, bringing with her the clothes and jewellery she had worn, and samples of the food that had been given to guests. Here, the class teacher is discussing Naseem's visit with a small group which includes bilingual children as well as speakers of English as a mother tongue:

33

Teacher:	*Do you remember when Naseem came in she brought some lovely food like she had had at her wedding? . . . Well, I've got some photographs of you eating it. Let's have a look at them.* (Pointing to a photograph.) *Can anyone tell me what that's called?*
Baljit:	*Chebra*
Seema:	*Chevra*
Baljit:	*Chebra*
Jayshree:	*Miss, miss, in Panjabi they say chebra and we say chevra. We say 'v' and they say 'b'.*
Baljit:	*Yes, . . . we say chebra and they say chevra.*
Teacher:	(turning to the whole group): *Let's try saying chevra first.* *(The children take turns to practise the word. There are various pronunciations, some of which elicit comments, laughs or corrections from other children.)*
Teacher:	*Who can tell me what it tastes like?*
Mark:	*It's quite hot and spicy.*
Teacher:	*Is it crunchy?*
Seema:	*Yes . . . it's got peanuts and some of those long things which are spicy. They're called gattia.*
Teacher:	*Called what?*
Children:	(in chorus) *Gattia . . . gattia G-att-i-a . . . gattia* (pronounces slowly and deliberately)
Seema:	*They're quite hot. And then there's peanuts . . .*
Jayesh:	*Kouru, they're called.*
Seema:	*Yes, kouru. Then there's rice and some brown things, they're quite hot . . .*
Jayesh:	*They're called . . . darr* (deliberately rolls the 'rs'). (The discussion continues with the children commenting on the various sweet and savoury foodstuffs, saying the names and occasionally negotiating over meanings.)
Teacher:	*What's this large one here?*
Jayshree:	*It begins with 'p' . . .*
Baljit:	(shouting) *Puri . . . puri* (The children practise the word around the group as before. They discuss the taste and texture of puri and eventually move on to something else.)
Teacher:	*What about* (points)? *. . .*
Jayesh:	*That's called ladoo.*
Teacher:	*Say it again?*

Children:	(in chorus) *Ladoo . . . ladoo . . . ladoo*
Baljit:	*We call it ludoo . . . l-u* (spells out the letters).
Seema:	*Not ludoo . . . ladoo.*
	(Discussion continues.)

Notice how willingly the children participate in the discussion; how they happily take on the teaching role, explaining to each other and their teacher the details of ingredients as well as the subtleties of pronunciation differences between their different languages.

We need to point out, however, that a lively classroom exchange like this cannot necessarily be expected to come about by chance. In most classes, as in this one, it involves careful advance planning by the teacher in order to ensure that the appropriate talking points are available. Most important is an atmosphere where the teacher is ready to learn from the pupils and the pupils know that their contributions will be welcomed. But, as we have seen, once that atmosphere has been established the benefits for the teacher, in terms of insight into children's cultural knowledge and linguistic awareness, are considerable.

Games

Much has been written elsewhere[5] about the value of games in developing cultural and linguistic awareness among children and we do not want to repeat this unnecessarily. In this section, therefore, we aim to show how you might adopt a self-help approach in your classroom by encouraging the children themselves to contribute their own and their families' knowledge of games in different languages and dialects.

A teacher in a class of 1st and 2nd year juniors found her starting point quite by chance when a boy of Bangladeshi background brought in a board game, Karee, from home. This sparked off a lot of discussion among the children about the games they liked and disliked. Soon afterwards Fortunata, one of the girls in the class, went off to Sicily to visit relatives. On her return a few weeks later she announced, 'I know a game . . . I learnt it from my cousins in Sicily.' She promptly demonstrated the game to the class and later wrote out the words in Sicilian dialect:

Ora, Dora
Ora ti bilancio
Quanto giorni a statio in Francia . . .
    uno, due, tre, quattro, cinque etc.. . .

which she was able to translate roughly into English:

Now, Dora
Now I'm checking up on you
How many days did you spend in France? . . .
    one, two, three, four, five etc. . . .

The teacher describes how the game can be played:

It is a game of elimination. Children can either stand in a ring, or put their right foot in a ring. Each foot is tapped by the leading child while everyone sings the rhyme. The last foot to be tapped chooses a number. The number is then counted around the ring of feet thus eliminating one foot every time.

It is the sort of 'dipping' game that appears all over the world in different cultures and no doubt you and pupils in your own class would be able to supply further examples.

'Ora Dora' became a firm playground favourite with the children in this school, so much so that the teacher used it to encourage other children to contribute their own games from their own cultures. With the help of parents the result was a pleasing collection of rhymes and rituals for eliminating, sorting, chasing and catching, all of which were eagerly tried by the children, eventually becoming a resource for the whole school to use.

Another teacher, with a class of older juniors, decided to explore a 'games' theme with a school assembly in mind:

We came together initially to discuss and play some well-known English games and the ideas flowed from there . . . we sorted out different types of games — indoor/outdoor, group/pairs/ individual, singing/moving, balls/bats etc. The children wrote out sets of rules for the games they knew. They described the games and illustrated the rhymes associated with them. Some were written out in as many as three languages.

The games we were teaching and learning began to appear and flourish in the playground and this led to even more games ideas coming from other classes. The wealth of material was unbelievable and we had a hard job cutting it down for our actual assembly.

Her conclusion was one that other teachers would share:

. . . we made a lot of discoveries about each other and about how much common ground there is in playing games. Any language or cultural barriers that may have existed between the children were soon broken down as children discovered that they played the same games, wherever their families originated from.

Songs, poems and rhymes

As suggested in the chart on page 15, songs, poems and rhymes have an important role to play in supporting language diversity in the multilingual classroom. Yet a first reaction to this idea may be one of scepticism. How can teachers, who are not themselves accomplished in the languages of their pupils, nor the musical forms of their cultures, possibly set about introducing activities that draw upon these?

Games I Like To Play

I like the game kho cause you have to run about alot and you get puffed out alot.

kabadi that is a nice game cause you have to hold your breath and still run about.

Langdi is a very nice game as well cause you have to hop in and try to catch people who are on two feet.

KO klashi is great fun cause you have to keep feeling with your hands at the back of you and then run.

king Ashoka is great fun as well but it is a bit rough.

I think all the games are great fun. I enjoy playing them very much.

by
. Minaxi Patel

KING ASHOKA

It has been a recurring theme of this chapter that in the normal classroom opportunities will regularly present themselves for teachers who wish to incorporate a multilingual dimension into their work. But for this to happen you must be alert to the potential of the opportunities as they arise. Here is an example of how one teacher's alertness provided her with an unexpected musical starting point:

My class of 5-7 year-olds were enjoying some rhymes when one child showed particular delight in the 'Hush-a-bye-baby' song. On the spur of the moment I sang them a simple German lullaby that I remembered. This prompted a young Lebanese boy to contribute the Arabic lullaby his mother sings for him and his sister; a girl from Venezuela sang a Spanish lullaby and a Sikh girl was eager to sing a Panjabi song picked up from her mother. Since then I have been able to record the Arabic lullaby onto tape, sung by Nasim's mother, with his father joining in . . .

The teacher hopes to develop this further by:

. . . collecting on the same tape French, German, Spanish, English, Panjabi, Bengali and Tamil songs from parents and friends. My plan is to write out the texts in English and the mother tongue with a simple transliteration. They will be put onto cards, similar to the Breakthrough to Literacy *set of rhymes we use regularly, with illustrations by the children. These cards will then be available for whole class use with the tape, or for private enjoyment in the listening corner.*

Other teachers have been anxious to encourage an exchange of language experiences at a whole school level and since musical activities are often occasions for bringing the whole school together they seemed a convenient area to focus upon. Here a teacher describes how this has been approached in her own school. She goes on to outline the value for bilingual children and indicates some of the many spin-off benefits at class level, including greater parental participation.

One way in which the whole school shares an interest in language variation is through music. The school meets together once a week for singing and music-making, using songs and music from a variety of cultural traditions. Songs with simple repetitive lines in different languages feature regularly. An overhead projector provides words and outline drawings for clues to comprehension. Actions, of course, add a dimension of enjoyment and give meaning to strange-sounding phrases.

38

Shamem and Namratta like this nursery song.

Future plans for the music session include small group workshops making instruments in traditional folk style and finding songs in languages to match with the help of parents and friends of the school.

Given the right encouragement bilingual children will themselves be able to contribute musically. Panjabi-speaking children have brought tapes of film music from home. Listening to the songs in small groups naturally stimulates talk about the films in which they feature, and the livelier the discussion the more likely it is to take place in Panjabi. In a mixed age group this can mean older children explaining the plot, action, relationships and characters to younger ones, and in a mixed language group Panjabi-speaking children can develop their skills of translation in an atmosphere of keen enjoyment. We have recorded children singing film songs as well as collecting soundtracks. We have played them while doing jigsaws or drawing, and interestingly, children who have not freely used their mother tongue in school, began to insert Panjabi words into their conversation about the jigsaws and their drawings.

A natural outcome of the children recording their own songs was one child volunteering his mother, who came to spend some time in the nursery and recorded songs and nursery rhymes in Gujarati.

Handling difficulties

In describing a method of working that clearly has been very successful and has enriched the curriculum in many ways, this teacher would not wish to shy away from some of the difficulties that have arisen. Below, she talks frankly about the difficulties that can arise when some children display hostility to other languages; difficulties that are not necessarily confined to music activities.

We include her comments, since the response of one school may provide practical help and encouragement to others who may see the danger of adverse pupil reaction as a deterrent to introducing aspects of language diversity.

We have had occasions when music from different cultural traditions has prompted embarrassment or ridicule, and given rise to stereotyped caricaturing. Reactions of children can be noted and, we feel, should be dealt with (usually more effectively) in the smaller class groups. Classroom work can relate to the themes and images of the music to validate it, and by making cultural and language variety a constant, and so a natural part of the classroom, we are working to overcome negative reactions.

In calling attention to some of the difficulties that can arise it may appear that we are introducing a negative note to the discussion. This is certainly not our intention. We are very aware of the many teachers who feel that so far the debate about multilingualism in education has tended to focus on the problems and difficulties, to the exclusion of the positive, exciting and enjoyable aspects of diversity. They would therefore like to see this book establish a sense of balance. At the same time, we know from teachers that problems do arise and there is a need for practical guidance on how these can be resolved. The example quoted, we feel, goes some way towards providing this guidance. It also serves as a fitting conclusion to this chapter as it brings us back to the points from which we started and which the chapter as a whole has tried to illustrate:

* learning about language diversity can become a natural and accepted feature of the classroom;
* it can permeate the curriculum as a whole, as well as being a worthwhile area of study in its own right;
* it is something to which bilingual and non-bilingual children can contribute;
* it can help all children towards a greater awareness of their own and each others' language experiences as well as the range of languages that go to make up our multicultural society.

3 Working with others in school and community

> *We like to think that in our school we have an open-door policy towards parents and the wider community. Being a multilingual school this means that we have all around us people who are bilingual in our pupils' languages and who have much to offer which can be of help in our work.*

There comes a point when teachers who do not speak the languages of their pupils will want to turn for assistance to people who are themselves bilingual and who might be prepared to make their skills available in some way to the school. Like the teacher quoted above you will probably be aware that there is a great deal of expertise of this sort in your own school and the wider community — parents, teachers in community mother tongue classes, secondary school students, school leavers, staffroom colleagues and others who work in the school, all of whom are potential sources of help in the classroom.

Asking others to put their skills at your disposal calls for tact and sensitivity as well as a great deal of mutual understanding. You cannot assume that their help and advice will always be offered readily. You should be prepared for discussion about the educational purpose behind your ideas, particularly the benefits for children. And once assistance is offered you should avoid taking it for granted or over-taxing the goodwill involved. In the case of bilingual parents, many of whom may be unfamiliar with the philosophy of primary schools and unaccustomed to having teachers seek their help, you should see this as part of your school's wider policy for improving channels of communication and establishing closer relations.

Contact with parents

Effective communication with parents and local communities has long been a major part of primary school practice; it is vital if children are to feel welcome and secure in school and if parents are to feel that they can make

41

their views known and have an opportunity to contribute to the work of the school. But where parents speak only a little English, and the school staff do not share the parents' language, communication is not easy[1].

In many schools much careful planning and thought has already gone into making communication possible. However, further discussion is essential if there is to be a two-way exchange, where parents feel their concerns for their children's education are respected and welcomed. The questions below, which have been prepared by a group of teachers in one authority, and the guidelines which follow, will provide a starting point from which teachers can begin to examine their own school's responses.

Sharing information about children on admission

* Who does the school admissions? Is there someone who can act as interpreter?
* What information is gathered?
* Does it include details of the language(s) spoken by the child, parents and siblings?
* Are admission forms multilingual? Are they sent out or given to parents in advance?
* What is the school policy on names?
* How are they pronounced and written?
* Does the school take account of different cultural and personal naming traditions?

In preparation for special events
* How and when are parents consulted about children taking part in school outings and events, especially where there might be religious or moral objections?
* How do parents inform staff about religious celebrations that might affect their children's attendance at school?
* In which sort of extra-curricular school activities do you seek parental support?
* How do you overcome language barriers?

Admissions procedures vary from school to school but as teachers become more aware of the importance of having a system that takes account of the needs of parents and children they sometimes see limitations in their existing arrangements.

> We felt that the collection of information about our children, including information about languages and cultural backgrounds, had been rather hit and miss and that the person collecting the information (the secretary) was not the person most suited to the task . . . We felt the first contact with the school should be a very positive and welcoming one.

As a first step, this school went on to change its admission form in order to include details of children's languages and religions as well as dietary needs. They then reviewed their admission procedure.

As most of our children start in the nursery, our admissions are now done by the person with responsibility for the nursery unit. She invites the parents and children into the nursery. She is then able to assist with the form-filling and explain why we need the information. The parents and children can also look round the nursery and ask questions . . . It gives the teachers a chance to form a good initial relationship with the parents and children and explain the nursery routine.

In other schools the Head may wish to have more direct involvement in admitting children and ensuring that a good rapport is established with parents from the outset. Whatever arrangement you follow, however, you should try to be certain that everybody involved in the admission process has guidance on dealing with parents.

Having access to someone who can act as an interpreter is important. Sometimes parents will bring along a friend or older child who will do the interpreting; and in some cases the school will be able to call on the services of a bilingual member of staff, a member of the local community or a local interpreting service.

Multilingual notices and letters with details of information needed on admission can be a useful resource to give or send to parents.

Important details

Certain details need to be collected with particular care and sensitivity because of varying practices across cultures, for example:

* Child's date of birth — the system for counting can vary between cultures.
* Child's and parents' names — can give rise to confusion when schools are not familiar with naming practices in different cultures.
* Diet and eating traditions — are important to know about, so that variations in school meals can be provided if necessary, and so that curriculum work on food can be handled sensitively.
* Religion — this information is vital not only so that teachers can understand the background of the child, but so that the parents are given an opportunity to discuss with teachers ways in which their religion is reflected in the work of the school. In some schools parents are invited to join school assemblies so that they can see what goes on for themselves; their decision as to whether they want their child to join in is then accepted as their right.

Sharing information about school policy and practice in print (school booklets, magazines, notices and letters)[2]
* How are these produced?
* If they are in multilingual versions, who does the translating and which dialect is used?
* What responses have you had from parents?
* How do you deal with negative or hostile reactions?
* How are leaflets, booklets etc. made available?
* What sort of notices do you have around your school?
* Where are they and how frequently are they changed?

Talking together (meetings at school, informal daily contact and home visiting)
* How are responsibilities for each of these shared among the school staff?
* What are the usual reasons for meetings with parents and home visiting?
* How much of a two-way exchange is possible and how can it be facilitated with parents of bilingual children?
* Have you introduced any procedures that enable parents to make constructive suggestions about school policy and practice?

As far as possible information about the school should be available in community languages, so that parents can ask for versions in their mother tongue. It is important, though, that when policy booklets and prospectuses are produced in other languages the layout and quality should conform with the English version.

Signs and notices in the languages of parents and children are now widely used in multilingual schools to accompany displays of work publicise forthcoming events, give directions for finding rooms and members of staff, or simply to welcome visitors. It is often difficult to ensure that signs used in the school are of uniform quality, but, whenever possible, schools should aim to achieve this.

Books/Library

When your children bring home books from school look at them with them and talk about the pictures in your home language.   Please help your child to look after books at home and return them to school.   Your local childrens' library will be happy to lend them books.

کتابیں / لائبریری

جب آپ کے بچے سکول سے کتابیں گھر لائیں، تو ان پر ایک نظر ڈال لیں، بلکہ کتابوں کی تصویروں پر بچوں کے ساتھ اپنی زبان میں تبادلہ خیال بھی کریں؛ مہربانی کرکے بچوں کو کتابیں اچھی حالت میں رکھنے کی تاکید کریں، اور وقت پر سکول واپس لے جانے کی عادت ڈالیں! آپ کے علاقے میں بچوں کی لائبریری، بچوں کو پڑھنے کے لئے کتابیں خوشی سے دے گی!

Journey to School

Bring your child to school yourself and show him/her how to get to school safely. Teach your child the Green Cross Code.   If your child travels to school by bus, wait and see your child safely onto the bus.

سکول جانا

اپنے بچے / بچی کو خود سکول چھوڑنے جائیے اور اس کو بتائیے کہ سکول پہنچنے کا محفوظ راستہ اور طریقہ کیا ہے۔ بچے کو "گرین کراس کوڈ" سکھائیے کہ سڑک کس طرح پار کی جاتی ہے۔ اگر آپ کا بچہ / بچی بس سے سکول جاتا ہے تو بس میں بحفاظت سوار ہونے تک اس پر نگاہ رکھیں۔

ਸਕੂਲ ਨੂੰ ਜਾਣਾ

ਤੁਸੀਂ ਆਪਣੇ ਬੱਚਿਆਂ ਨੂੰ ਆਪ ਸਕੂਲ ਛੱਡਣ ਜਾਇਆ ਕਰੋ ਤੇ ਉਨ੍ਹਾਂ ਨੂੰ ਸਿਖਾਓ ਕਿ ਸਕੂਲ ਬਚਾਅ ਨਾਲ ਕਿਵੇਂ ਜਾਣਾ ਹੈ। ਬੱਚੇ ਨੂੰ ਗਰੀਨ ਕਰਾਸ ਕੋਡ ਸਿਖਾਓ। ਜੇਕਰ ਤੁਹਾਡਾ ਬੱਚਾ ਬੱਸ ਤੇ ਜਾਵੇ ਤਾਂ ਉਸ ਨੂੰ ਬੱਸ ਵਿਚ ਬਿਠਾ ਕੇ ਜਾਓ।

As with all aspects of using the mother tongue, such initiatives have to be carefully discussed with parents. You may be inclined to try to avoid this as some English-speaking parents in your school might be known to be hostile to any form of cultural or linguistic diversity.

Unfortunately a number of English parents were not happy about us celebrating Diwali and withdrew their children from school for the day. They said they didn't want their children involved in any act of worship other than a Christian one . . . Other parents, although not withdrawing their children, did not approve and in fact spread malicious rumours insinuating that there were to be no Christmas celebrations in school and that we were only interested in the Asian children.

In addition there might be bilingual parents who feel instinctively that their children should have maximum exposure to English.

> *. . . The general feeling among the ethnic minority parents was very strong — they didn't want anything to make their children different. They felt that in England they should read, write and think in English.*

Whilst not wishing to deny the strength of these reactions nor the disheartening effect they can have on teachers, you should be prepared to respond to them. There will, of course, always be some parents who will remain unconvinced by what you have to say. But we have found that an educational explanation of what you are doing will be well received by many parents, especially if it is backed up with evidence of how children are benefiting, and promptly followed up with an invitation to see your approach at work in the classroom.

Teachers sometimes find that adverse reaction from parents is more likely to happen when the parents are not only unfamiliar with the work of the school but also unaccustomed to meeting their children's teachers. This is one of the reasons why regular informal contact between parents and teachers is now becoming a feature of life in many primary schools. It often takes place as opportunities arise in the classroom, at the school gates or in the street. It gives teachers and parents a valuable means of discussing matters of mutual interest and of becoming better acquainted with each other, thus helping to establish a relationship of trust and understanding.

Home visits, too, are now becoming a part of this way of working, although there is still a tendency for them to be associated with sorting out problems rather than the more positive aspects of children's school activities. Contact in the home is being found by some teachers to be particularly important in encouraging bilingual parents, who may have very little to do with the school, to become more actively involved in their children's learning. Not surprisingly, more class teachers are coming to recognise that visiting pupils' families is not just the responsibility of the home-school liaison teacher. It is something to be shared among all members of staff. With this in mind some schools are now beginning to evolve arrangements for class teachers regularly to be released from teaching duties.

Sharing responsibility for learning in school

Talking about the work and progress of individual children
* What channels of contact are available for such discussion to take place?
* How can contact be improved where there is a language difference?

Sharing expertise within the school curriculum
* How can parents contribute to aspects of your school curriculum, given the constraints of full-time work and differences in teaching

methodology?

* How can you help all parents to feel involved in your work on linguistic diversity and in the multicultural curriculum generally?

Parental and community involvement can be an invaluable resource in developing educational responses to bilingual children and in introducing all children to diverse forms of language. But for this to become an effective way of working in the classroom, teachers need to be sensitive in their approaches to parents and in the assistance they ask of them. Individual parents cannot be thought of, for example, as being representative of their linguistic or cultural groups. They may have differing views on the extent to which they want to share their linguistic experience with schools and this needs to be respected. And where parents or other community members become involved in the classroom, teachers may find that they need to exercise caution, so as to avoid making excessive demands on them — demands that could so easily amount to exploitation of an unpaid educational resource.

In practice — a summary of ideas

In practice, many teachers have successfully worked with parents and members of their local communities. The flow chart on page 48, based on teachers' own lists of how they have drawn upon parental and community language expertise, illustrates the many valuable contributions that have been made.
The chart could be used as a basis for discussion among teachers who are beginning to consider how they might work more closely with their local communities. In schools where such approaches are already under way, the chart might be a helpful means of monitoring the extent of community participation and identifying future lines of development.

Two case studies — junior and nursery

There are two accounts by teachers of different ways in which parents have helped schools respond to the languages of their pupils. The first was in a junior school.

We wanted to be able to provide weekly half-hour story sessions in Urdu, Panjabi, Gujarati and/or Hindi. We had storybooks in all these languages.

On Parents' Evening a notice in English and Urdu, plus photos of story sessions in progress, was displayed; parents were asked to speak to the Head or to the E2L teacher who is an Urdu-speaker.

One mother showed interest. She was visited by the home-school liaison teacher and agreed to come regularly to tell and read stories.

In the sessions, since all the children are either Pakistani Panjabi speakers or Sikh Panjabis, but conversant with Urdu, she operates in Urdu, when reading, and in Panjabi, when speaking. Thus she can check children's comprehension as she goes along.

Children have shown great interest, and parents from other language groups are now offering their assistance.

PARENTS AND LOCAL COMMUNITIES CAN USE THEIR LANGUAGES TO HELP WITH . . .

Games and rhymes

Teaching games and rhymes to children

Recording rhymes on tape

Craft and cookery

Writing recipes

Cookery sessions with children

Sewing and other crafts

Stories

Telling stories to children

Recording stories on tape

Encouraging children to write mother tongue stories

Music and drama

Helping with dramatic productions

Teaching dance

Recording songs on tape

Teaching songs to children

Translating

Signs, labels and notices

Children's own stories and writing

Books for children

Letters and circulars

Play activities

In the home play area

With sand and water

With constructional toys

Number work

Displays of numbers and counting systems

Counting activities with children

Making games and work cards

The second was in a nursery school where the teacher wanted to develop classroom strategies for encouraging greater parental involvement.

I wanted to try out a project that all children could contribute to. The theme 'babies' seemed to be a good one — all the children would be able to participate by bringing a photograph of themselves as babies, and I could introduce it at a time in the term when new parents were staying in the classroom to settle children. Some of these parents would be able to share each others' 'baby' experiences.

I began with a display of baby things, one side of which was for photographs, including baby photos of myself and my colleague. Small discussion groups of children looked at the photos. The parents enjoyed seeing the likeness between us and our photos. They soon began to bring photographs to contribute to the display and this seemed to encourage much greater mixing between the parents themselves as they joined us in discussions about the photographs.

Additional work was organised in the home corner where parents helped in feeding and bathing the dolls, changing their nappies, etc. The baby of an Icelandic girl was bathed by mum in the classroom with the whole class watching. As a next step we propose exploring how babies are fed and weaned in different cultures. And we are hoping soon to be able to visit the local baby clinic.

Community mother tongue classes

Although many schools have now made considerable progress towards establishing a close working partnership with parents, the same cannot be said of their relationships with local community mother tongue classes, some of which make use of the same school premises at evenings and weekends[3]. This is particularly unfortunate in view of the substantial experience that exists in community classes and the important role that they often play in the lives of bilingual children and their families.

A starting point for any links between you and your local community mother tongue classes must be that you share a concern for the development of children's bilingualism and that there is much you can learn from each other. As a first step in making contact you could:

* find out from your pupils which classes they attend, where they are and when they operate.
* try visiting the classes to meet the teachers and see the work that is taking place. You could arrange this by sending a letter with one of the children or by simply calling round.

Once you have a rapport with the teachers, which may require two or three visits, you could begin to discuss ways of collaborating. The following ideas might be helpful[4]:

* occasional meetings (one a term?) between the community teachers and you and your mainstream colleagues, in order to discuss teaching aims, methods and materials;

* shared use of teaching resources and facilities (e.g., books/ classroom apparatus and reprographic/audio-visual equipment);
* providing mutual advice on the production and purchase of teaching materials;
* exchanging knowledge and expertise (e.g., through games, songs, stories);
* developing joint resources such as packs of teaching materials and stories on tape;
* following joint teaching themes or organising joint activities (e.g., at festival times).

No doubt you could add to this list, but the important thing to remember is that any relationship between the mainstream and community sectors should be one of equals. This means that you should be careful about appearing to be imposing your own approaches onto community teachers who may have long experience in the field and their own preferred teaching methods. Any contact between you, then, should be based on mutual respect for each others' expertise and a recognition of the complementary roles that both sectors play in the lives of bilingual children.

Secondary school students

Bilingual secondary school students can make a helpful contribution in multilingual primary schools. An example of this type of work is currently being developed in one authority as an element in a general scheme of involvement in primary schools. Secondary students are placed in local primary schools as teachers' aides for half a day per week. The students, initially under close teacher supervision, work with small groups of children using the children's mother tongue, telling them stories and leading discussion arising from these. They also often act as interpreters for children, staff and parents. Teachers have found that these secondary students can play an important part in raising awareness of linguistic diversity in the classroom and school. As Heads and teachers have commented:

> *The objectives were that the children would see their own language and customs welcomed and respected in their school and would feel less alienated from the school environment. We felt that this was achieved, and that the children were happier and achieved more in school. They were all more forthcoming and more prepared to discuss their own home life with us.*
>
> *The project achieved a great deal in our school. Staff felt they understood far more about the children at the end of it. We all learnt a great deal . . . the children were prepared to talk about Asian customs in assembly without embarrassment. The children chose mother tongue story tapes when available. They were prepared to translate for other children who needed help.*

Asian mothers were prepared to come to school for an Asian dance event giving us an idea for involving them in school activities.

In many ways we are asking the impossible from these young people, but it is heartening to see how well they cope; many newly qualified teachers with four years' training sometimes experience similar difficulties.

With any scheme of this nature there are likely to be some difficulties. These will arise mainly from some of the students' lack of confidence and experience. In these circumstances some initial preparation on the part of the school is crucially important if the students are to make a full contribution and derive some satisfaction from the experience.

Some points to bear in mind

* The students will need preparation to enable them to understand the purposes of the work and to approach the tasks in an appropriate way with the children.
* The students will find it easier to work regularly with the same small group of children.
* Throughout, class teachers should be closely involved with the work that takes place.
* Class teachers should meet regularly with the students to discuss the progress of the work and to offer guidance when needed.

Overall, there are considerable potential benefits to schemes of this nature, not only for the bilingual children and their teachers, but also for the students themselves who are given positive and creative opportunities to use their mother tongue skills.

Bilingual teachers

Teachers who speak children's mother tongues are among the most valuable resources available to multilingual schools. Often these teachers perform a wide range of functions over and above their normal duties as class teachers — liaising with parents and the community, counselling, advising other teachers, acting as interpreters and translators, etc. Many are pleased to work in this way and to offer their expertise to the school. Nevertherless, we feel there are some points that schools should bear in mind:

* When bilingual staff are employed as normal class teachers there is sometimes a tendency to ask them to act in a bilingual capacity in their spare time. It is important that proper recognition be given to their specialist language skills, and their role as translators, interpreters and counsellors.
* When a school identifies an educational case for bilingual class teachers this needs to be incorporated into staff policy. The school's particular needs should be mentioned in job advertisements and information about language skills should be elicited during interviews.
* When schools feel that there is a case for bilingual specialists who are not involved as full-time class teachers it is important that, where possible, appropriate staffing appointments are made or LEA specialist services called upon.

Bilingual aides

Classroom aides do not exist in all LEAs and even in those areas of the country where there is provision for them to be appointed there is by no means unanimity among teachers about their value. Nevertheless, there now seems to be a tendency for more authorities to make these posts available to schools. Not surprisingly, then, some Headteachers in multicultural areas are seeing this as a further opportunity to appoint bilingual adults to the school's staff and thus make more support available to class teachers and bilingual pupils.

In one authority these aides have a specific brief to assist in the schools' language development programmes. We therefore felt it would be of interest to include a Headteacher's account of the contribution that a bilingual aide has been able to make to the school's policy of mother tongue development.

> *Before the children are admitted to school they visit individually with their parents. The aide acts as interpreter for the parents and for the member of staff who will help the child to settle into school.*
>
> *I had always felt that the children who had most difficulty in learning English were those who were not fluent in their own language, but I had no means of checking. When the aide was appointed I learnt that this feeling was correct. When new non-English-speaking children have become settled in school and feel happy with other adults the aide then works with them in their mother tongue to ascertain their degree of fluency. She also makes note of any speech difficulty.*
>
> *If children are not fluent in their mother tongue I discuss this with their parents with the help of the aide. We then explain that the aide will give their children extra help in the mother tongue. The initial reaction is often 'We have sent our child to school to learn English', but when it is explained that the child will learn English more quickly if s/he is more fluent in the mother tongue, the parents are then most co-operative and borrow books from the school library to look at with their children.*
>
> *I find it essential to have an Asian member of staff who speaks several languages. This is not only important for the reasons already stated, but children and parents can also see that we have a respect for their religions and cultures as well as languages.*

It is apparent that in this particular school the bilingual aide has become a mainstay of the school's liaison programme with parents as well as its provision for mother tongue learning. No doubt this model will be of interest to other schools that are considering making similar appointments. If your school is in this position there are a number of matters that you should discuss carefully:

* Interpreting between teachers and parents is a specialist responsibility. How best can you prepare a bilingual aide for this?
* What training should you provide to help a bilingual aide work effectively with children through the medium of the mother tongue?
* Is there any role for a bilingual aide in assessing children's mother tongue fluency? If so, what training is needed for this?
* How can you prepare a bilingual aide to explain to parents the importance of maintaining their children's mother tongue?

Other bilingual adults

There may be other bilingual adults working in the school. Caretakers, cleaners and kitchen staff, for example, can all play an important part in the school's positive response to the languages of its pupils.

You may wish to think about how best to draw upon the skills of such people and how to give them any necessary reassurance that it is valuable to talk with children in the mother tongue.

Some final points

Having given some advice on the sources of bilingual expertise to which you could turn, there are some final points we would like to make by way of guidance on working with parents and other community volunteers:

* it is important that volunteers know the purpose of the activity in which they are being asked to help;
* if working with children they will need to know whether it will be limited to children from their own language group, or if other children will also be involved;
* they may need some guidance on story-telling techniques, operating classroom equipment and using materials;
* a useful way of providing guidance may be through a preparatory session where the volunteer is able to work alongside a teacher and see him/her using similar techniques, equipment or materials;
* you should remember that parents and community volunteers cannot be substitutes for qualified teachers;
* they are more likely to see themselves as having certain skills that they are happy to make available for a specific purpose and a limited period of time;
* few helpers would feel able to enter into a long-term commitment to the school and may be embarrassed to find teachers becoming over-dependent on them;
* as a long-term measure, then, whilst continuing to encourage community participation, you may wish to approach your LEA or Multicultural Support Service with a view to obtaining the assistance of a professional interpreter/translator and a qualified bilingual teacher.

4 Collecting and using mother tongue stories

> *For most teachers in our school, stories in the mother tongue have been the easiest way of making a start on valuing the children's languages.*

Using stories is an integral part of the primary school curriculum, and story time is a regular part of the day when pupils come together to enjoy a common experience. In multilingual classes the use of mother tongue stories is a natural extension of existing practice, and a particularly valuable way of responding to the skills and experiences which children bring with them to school. It can help in:

* giving status to the languages children speak;
* confirming that children's languages and cultures are valued by the teacher;
* supporting bilingual children's English language learning;
* increasing all children's interest in different forms of language;
* strengthening relationships between school, parents and the wider community;
* extending all children's understanding of different cultures.

Many teachers now recognise the value of introducing story material that reflects the mother tongues of their pupils. Often, like the school that supplied the quote at the start of this section, this has been approached with great enthusiasm and is seen as the most obvious starting point from which to develop a more comprehensive response to language diversity. But, despite their enthusiasm, teachers still have many questions:

* How should I go about selecting mother tongue stories?
* Where can I get help with translation?
* How can I set about producing stories myself?
* What do I need to bear in mind when using mother tongue stories in the classroom?

Later in this section we offer some guidelines that go some way towards answering these and other questions.

Mother tongue story telling — some approaches for the classroom

A story dramatised and photographs or slides taken which can then be used as a basis for a written version.

A bilingual teacher, parent or secondary student, telling a story in the mother tongue and then the same story being told in English to the whole class.

Sequential photographs of children engaged in an activity such as a school trip, made into a book with dual text.

Translated versions of books made from individual children's stories.

Taped stories, with or without written versions, included in listening corners.

A story dramatised and presented in English and the mother tongue in a school assembly.

Making a video recording of a dramatised story and using this as a school resource.

A picture book story told in the mother tongue with the aid of puppets, cut-outs or magnet board figurines, to enable all children to follow it.

Making class books of stories round a theme, such as 'water stories' or 'stories about weddings' where the children can draw from their differing experiences.

The use of older children in the school to tell young children stories in the mother tongue.

A simple story, with good visual clues, which two children speaking different languages can use working as a pair.

A chart — some approaches

We begin with a chart that outlines some of the various ways in which teachers have introduced mother tongue story-telling into their classrooms. Some of the approaches are then examined in more detail through individual teachers' accounts of work they have undertaken with their pupils.

56

There are many schools and individual teachers who have begun to develop their own approaches along some of the lines indicated on the chart. Typical of these are the two examples that follow.

The first comes from an infant school where live and taped story-telling sessions were introduced, based on books that were already available in the children's mother tongues. Two books published by the Children's Book Trust of New Delhi[1] proved particularly successful — the Gujarati and English editions of Shobana and the Gujarati and Bengali editions of The Elephant and the Mice. In both cases the stories were told and recorded in the mother tongue by parents.

With Shobana, in line with normal infant practice, the children engaged in a range of follow-up activities.

> *The story was acted in drama sessions. Colour slides of the main points of the story were taken during the sessions. A large, almost life-size Indian cow and calf were produced in school to show the differences between them and the cows seen in farms near the school. Sticky paper pictures of the main characters were produced during art and craft activities.*

Yet despite the popularity and undoubted success of the stories, the school reports two recurring areas of difficulty:

> *. . . ensuring that the recordings of the stories were accurate and in a form of language that the children could understand . . . and coping with the reluctance of some of the children to use their mother tongues during the sessions.*

The second example also highlights some of the difficulties that can arise in this way of working.

> *One of the teachers who specialised in E2L in the school was interested in using tapes in the children's mother tongue. The BBC tape of* The Mice and the Elephants[2] *was played to Pakistani Muslim children in what was thought to be a language close to their mother tongue. However, the children could not understand it as their language was a particular regional dialect and the taped story was in a more standard variety.*
>
> *The teacher then decided to try to get some simple English stories translated by a parent and the next step was to find a person who was both willing and capable, and someone who could translate from reading into speech in an interesting way. The parent who was asked spoke the dialect of most of the children in the community and could also read, write and speak English fluently. He was provided with a cassette and said he could borrow a good tape recorder to record the stories. The parent was given two stories to record,* The Enormous Turnip *and* The Little Red Hen *and was also provided with a chime bar*

to strike each time he turned over a page. He took about three weeks to complete the translations.

The teacher then used the tape with several groups of children from reception to top infant. She found that with the older children they had a positive boost on hearing their language and wanted to tell the teacher what the story was about, whilst younger children found it difficult to concentrate.

The need for preparation

Even from these two short accounts it is becoming clear that successful use of mother tongue stories in the classroom depends on teachers being carefully prepared and anticipating some of the difficulties that can arise. Our third example reinforces this point by showing how one teacher set about planning her story sessions and dealing with some of the practical issues that for others have caused disappointment and frustration. In her case the result was a series of story sessions that were rewarding for the children and stimulating for the teacher.

My aim was to include bilingual story-telling as part of the everyday infant curriculum. The 'live' story-telling session is the best means of presentation where the meaning of the story is supported and enriched by facial expressions, eye contact, gestures, and where the story is paced and amplified to meet the needs of the listening children. There is no substitute for the live story-telling session. However, if schools have not yet acquired the necessary expertise, a useful starter might be the provision of 'listening corners', with stories on tape with headphones.

Choosing the stories

I decided to offer folk stories, with clear story lines and referring to contexts and notions likely to be understood by urban-living infants and also preferably involving dialogue with repetition.

The sources of the stories are authentic traditional tales such as can be found in the Panchatantra *— these stories have been passed down for generations in the pleasurable 'grandparent's knee' situation. The same plots turn up in collections all over the world to teach about the meaning of human life. They can be discovered in bookshops, newsagents and libraries, or they can be ordered from publishers and agents in this country.*

I chose stories that seemed to have humorous elements and with an ideological content appealing to very young people. For example, 'small can be powerful', 'thinking is more effective than brute force'.

Most of the folk stories involved animals — crocodiles, elephants, tigers, rabbits — all well known, but the context of 'country' or 'jungle' was more difficult to convey. Several stories we tried included topographical features, like 'river bank' or 'path through jungle', and on questioning, it was evident that the little children had not understood these critical elements in the story. They were just 'getting the gist of it', yet they gave every evidence of appreciating the plot — laughing and reacting appropriately.

Pictures are essential, particularly at the primary stage, to focus attention and provide further clues to meaning. Booklets of picture illustrations to the story were provided in the 'listening corner' and for teachers to use when presenting the story.

Story telling

I was fortunate in gaining the help of Gita who is proficient in English and Gujarati (a member of our local Interpreting and Translating Service), and who soon developed a good story-telling technique.

For the Panjabi stories we were lucky to have a bilingual teacher in the school, who was convinced of the value of the bilingual approach. All the stories were also recorded in English.

Procedure

The routine was that I chose a story — I tried to have consultations with the teacher about the choice each week, but this proved to be difficult. Teachers had copies and they did their best to find chances to tell it in English with a picture book so that the children didn't come to the story 'cold'.

Having chosen the story, Gita translated it 'straight' into English, and I then modified the story to simplify the language. I tried to do this without losing the characterisation, the descriptive bits, the sequence of the story, etc. Gita then made a translation back into Gujarati. We consulted a lot at first about certain words which would be outside their usage, whether to teach the Gujarati words for tiger, for instance.

Story time

We worked with 5–7-year-olds. Gita wore a tie-clip microphone whilst telling the children the story.

She checked first to make sure they knew, for instance, the Gujarati word for crocodile, etc. The recording was made with reference to page numbers so that it could be taken directly and used in listening corners. The recording, with giggles and gasps

and comments, was very much appreciated by the children who recognised their own interventions when hearing the tape. I believe that this 'unclean' tape is attractive and meaningful to young children.

Some comments
Many pieces of learning came my way. The Muslim children speak a different kind of Gujarati than the Hindu Gujarati children. Those children whose parents came from Africa — Uganda, for instance — have many Swahili words in their vocabulary.

All the children now rightly use many English words and idioms in their Gujarati, and this must be taken account of when choosing various possible versions.

A teacher who may think a story 'too difficult' for the children because it is too difficult in English, the second language, may be surprised to find that it is understood when heard first in Gujarati.

Several of even the youngest children had better fluency in English than Gujarati; for them it was already a case of 'retrieving' their mother tongue.

The Panjabi children like to listen to the Gujarati tape and vice versa. Several of the little children appeared to understand Hindi, Panjabi and Gujarati and certainly many junior-aged children are orally proficient in three languages.

As these examples have shown, using stories in the mother tongue has the potential to be a satisfying and exciting activity for both teacher and pupils. But it is equally capable of having the reverse effect. If it is to succeed, then it requires a great deal of preparation and forethought.

With this in mind, we now set out some guidelines to help you in selecting, translating, producing and using mother tongue stories. These are based on detailed discussions among teachers in one particular authority but they reflect many of the concerns raised by teachers elsewhere.

Selection

For teachers who do not share the languages of their pupils the choice of stories in the mother tongue is often very difficult. A number of points need to be borne in mind:

* Teachers need to be careful that their enthusiasm for valuing children's languages does not lead them to suspend the judgement that they would normally apply in selecting story material for classroom use. So, factors such as interest level, appeal of illustrations, length, linguistic level, quality of print and binding need to be considered, as do questions of cultural relevance, race bias and sex bias. To help with this you may find it useful to refer to one of the several published guides[3].
* Who chooses the story? Usually teachers themselves; but if you have little experience of your pupils' cultural backgrounds you may wish to encourage the children to make their own selections. For nursery and infant children, parents could be consulted as they may have ideas of particular favourites. If the school has access to a teacher who speaks one of the languages concerned then she or he could also be asked for advice.
* Which type of story? Folk-tales have been a useful resource for teachers wishing to develop mother tongue stories, not least because they provide opportunities for children to explore how similar themes appear in different cultures. But children born in Britain will sometimes have only a scanty knowledge of the cultural practices of their parents' or grandparents', country of origin. Their cultural experience may be quite different to that presented in a traditional folk-tale. To avoid difficulties in this area you may prefer to select stories about the children's own contemporary experiences which they can share with their classmates.
* Teachers wishing to use a story to help the English language development of bilingual children could choose one of the many titles which are popular with younger children, preferably with clear illustrations and repeating sequences. If the story is retold in the mother tongue, then the bilingual children will become familiar with the storyline and so can participate more fully in story sessions.

To underline the importance of careful selection a teacher of 5–7-year-olds recounts her own experience:

*Vimal, a Panjabi-speaking Adult Literacy Tutor, volunteered to
read the children a story written in Panjabi. When I saw the book
I was a little worried because it had a lot of print and very few
illustrations, all of which were in black and white . . . The
children's reactions confirmed my fears. The older ones tended
to sit still but the younger ones fidgeted and appeared bored after
a few minutes. The content seemed too advanced for them and it
was in a form of Panjabi that they did not understand.*

This question of finding the most appropriate form of the language has
concerned many teachers. We will now touch upon it as we discuss how
you can set about getting stories translated into the mother tongue.

Translation

* How to get help with translation? Some LEAs have a translation unit
  which schools can use. But when making use of this facility you
  should always explain to the translators the age of the children the
  story is aimed at, to help them choose the most appropriate style
  and register.
* If you do not have access to a service like this, you may find that
  parents and members of the local community are ready to help.
  Many teachers have found this very useful but, remember, when
  using voluntary help you cannot expect the sort of quick response
  which you would demand of a professional. You must also be wary
  of imposing impossible tasks on people who are already very busy
  and possibly too polite to say 'no'.
* Which type of language should you use? This is especially important
  if a teacher wants to have stories on tape as well as a written record.
  Very few bilingual pupils speak the standard version of their mother
  tongue, just as few English speakers grow up speaking standard
  English as their first language. We have known this question arise
  for teachers whose pupils speak any one of several mother tongues
  — Cypriot Greek, Sylheti Bengali, Mirpuri Panjabi, Kutchi and
  Sicilian Italian. One teacher, by way of an experiment, played to her
  class of older juniors a story in Urdu and Mirpuri Panjabi. Although
  they understood the Urdu version, their responses told her which
  was most comfortable for them:

That's our language . . . . . . it's Panjabi.

Other teachers have preferred to take the advice of parents or
bilingual colleagues. Our experience is that if tapes only are required
then the dialect will probably be more suitable for the children. If you
wish to have tapes and a written form then you should consider
having both in the standard variety.

Production and presentation

* Who produces the final version of the story and how should it be presented?
* If you are using taped material you should make sure that the story is presented in a way which will engage the children's interest and attention. A story read flatly and boringly, albeit in the mother tongue, will still be flat and boring. So whoever does the taped version should be able not only to read well, but also to engage the children's interest by the tone and timbre of the voice.

When considering the production of books in the mother tongue there are several questions to be resolved:

* Typescript or handwriting? You may find that a local community centre or community newspaper has a suitable typewriter available. This could help you prepare a very professional finished product. The Bengali text below was produced on a typewriter and then enlarged on a photocopying machine.

একটা ছোট ছেলে হাতি আর একটা ছোট মেয়ে হাতি।

বাবা হাতি আর মা হাতি।

If you decide to use handwriting then issues of size, clarity and correctness will need to be discussed with whoever is to do it. But here, too, good results can be achieved.
* Should the book be bilingual or monolingual? This depends on the purpose of the story. If bilingual children are working on the same story as their English-speaking peers you may decide that a bilingual version is needed.
  In other cases you may feel that a monolingual mother tongue version is more appropriate.
* Should the book have a transliteration? Teachers often find that by including a Roman script transliteration of a mother tongue text they can make a book 'readable' by more children and adults.
* Above all, when developing any materials in the languages of bilingual pupils care should be taken at every stage to ensure that the end product is of a standard which will enhance the status of the languages.

Use in the classroom

* You may want to use a story as a class activity which encourages the bilingual children to use English as well as their mother tongue.

Marianne Quartararo

Two six-year-olds (Chinese and Vietnamese) made up a story about two dragons who couldn't understand each other's languages. The children helped the dragons to learn each other's language! They put the story in a book with help from home to write phrases such as 'Hello' and 'What's the matter?' in the mother tongue. They then recorded the story on tape in English. The idea developed into a spate of dragon stories by the whole class, and a dragon wall display.

* Or you may want to give others in the class an opportunity to become more aware of other languages. Indeed teachers have often been surprised at the reactions of English speakers, like the teacher of 5–6-year-olds who reported:

I was surprised that the English children were so interested in the story. It was the first time they had listened to a story in a different language told without English translations. Three days later Maureen said 'I liked that story about Rupa the Elephant'.

After the story my bilingual colleague went on to teach the children a rhyme in Panjabi. She then asked them to try saying 'My name is . . .' in Panjabi.

* If story time comes during the day, rather than at the end, then props such as figurines, objects and puppets used by the teacher can be used again by the children to retell the story in English or the mother tongue.

* If the story is part of a project the teacher may group speakers of the same language to work together and then report back to the rest of the class. Folk stories and poems particularly lend themselves to activities of this sort.

Getting the most out of a story

To round off this section we show some of the variety of ways in which teachers have interpreted the idea of mother tongue story-telling in order to support further skills among their pupils and to expand into other areas of the curriculum[4]. This account comes from a 5–11 primary school:

Junior children made a tape recording of the story Rupa the Elephant[5] *in the different languages they knew. The completed tape has versions in English, Gujarati, Mirpuri, Bengali, Panjabi and Chinese.*

The idea arose from the thinking of the Head of infants, who said that she would like to have taped stories, suitable for infant children, told in different languages, so that bilingual children could listen first to a story in their home language and then in English. An accompanying picture book of the story would help the understanding of both languages.

A club for third and fourth year junior children was introduced. Groups were formed from children who spoke a common language other than English. Everyone had a copy of the story in English, and the whole group discussed the story and its characters. It was decided that each of the animal characters in the story should say more than they did in the written original, so that each member of the group could become one, or more, of the

65

animal voices. It was also decided that the translations into home languages should not attempt to be word for word, but should simply aim to preserve the essential meaning of the story. Words which the children did not know, or could not find out about, or for which there was no equivalent in the particular home language, could be retained in English if the group felt that they were necessary.

The children were the experts as the individual group discussions about the translations progressed. The teacher's role, since he had the disadvantage of speaking only in English, was to act as facilitator, encouraging decisions to be made about finalising the characters, calling for opinions about the accuracy of translation from other members of the group, encouraging thought about the pace, pitch and clarity of the narrators and so on. There seemed to be some good lessons to be learned here about the nature of the teacher's role in other discussions with children.

A number of interesting points have emerged:

* *none of the language groups re-wrote or altered the original script in its written form. The tape recordings themselves were made using only the English copies as aids to the telling of the story in a different language — remarkable skill on the part of the translators if you consider that not only some of the words themselves but also the structure and pattern of words in a sentence needed to be changed. The children involved were pleased to have the opportunity to display these skills and the permanency of the recording gave a new status and prestige to the languages.*

* *One of the groups had a number of children for whom other areas of the curriculum held some difficulties. This group proved to have the greatest expertise in this activity. Their preparation took the shortest time and the recordings they made had a fluency which earned the admiration of the other groups. There has since been a corresponding change in the outlook of the children in this group towards other school activities.*

* *Two children who had recently been admitted to school speaking only Bengali were able to make a full contribution to the tape through the help of speakers of Bengali and English.*

As a follow-up to the completed tape, the children involved with its production will listen to the story versions with infant children and discuss with them their understanding of the story.
In this way they will be able to make their own assessment of the value of the tape and decide what, if any, revisions are needed.

In a class of 9–10 year olds, a Chinese girl who had arrived in England two terms previously was asked by her teacher to translate a Chinese story into English and to make it into a book which could be shared with others. The follow-up activities took a number of directions, all involving the whole class.

> *. . . painting the Chinese way, reading the Willow Pattern story, paper folding, making kites, fans and lanterns, working with Chinese puzzles and tangrams, a visit by Korean and Thai ladies with costumes and artefacts to show the children, learning some Chinese phrases in small groups . . . The whole thing ended with a Chinese meal eaten in school and cooked by the girl's father.*

For our final example, the chart below shows how a teacher of 4–6-year-olds, most of whom were Panjabi speakers, expanded a bilingually-presented story into a class topic. Her starting point was *The Banyan Tree* [6]:

THE BANYAN TREE

Writing
grouping animals from story

ordering groups

simple sentences (English/Panjabi) for class book of the story

English/Panjabi picture dictionary of animals

Story-telling
listening to story on tape (English/Panjabi)

children retelling story on tape (English/Panjabi)

Class discussion about characters and events in story (English)

Art
model of the Banyan Tree

cut out shapes of animals from story

animals positioned in tree with labels (Panjabi/ English)

Maths
mapping groups to numerals (English/ Panjabi)

block graph of different animals from story

measuring height of class-made Banyan Tree

---

5 Learning and using your pupils' languages

At the beginning and end of each school day I try to make a point of saying something to the children in at least one of their languages.

It is now quite common to meet teachers who, like the Headteacher quoted above, have gone some way towards learning and using some everyday vocabulary and a few key phrases in one or more of the languages spoken by their pupils. Often this is done informally, as opportunities arise during normal class activities, with the teacher simply asking children or parents to teach him/her the words for common items and the phrases for greetings and simple questions. Increasingly, though, we are finding that some teachers are choosing to extend their knowledge further by taking advantage of evening courses that are available in the LEAs for learning community languages.

Some difficulties

Of course, to learn another language, even just a smattering of vocabulary and phrases, is not without its difficulties — some of which are of a practical nature:

* In a classroom where several languages are spoken it may not be easy to decide which to learn.
* You may not always have access to a bilingual speaker who is able to give you the assistance you want.
* Learning another language to any depth requires perseverance, practice and, above all, time. As a busy class teacher you may find this latter commodity in very short supply.

There are linguistic considerations to think about:

* Many children will speak a regional variety, such as Mirpuri or Sylheti, which has no written script. You will need to decide whether it is this you wish to focus upon or, if you want to become literate in the language, whether the standard form will be more appropriate.

There is always a need for care and sensitivity:

* Children can sometimes become acutely embarrassed at being asked to demonstrate their language skills, especially if the subject is introduced abruptly.
* Most parents are unaccustomed to having a close relationship with their children's teachers and so, understandably, they may be hesitant about taking on the role you are asking of them.
* They may feel it patronising to be spoken to in their mother tongue by a person with only the most superficial knowledge of it.
* Some may regard your interest as an intrusion into their private worlds.

However, despite the difficulties, in view of the importance that some teachers are beginning to attach to this aspect of their work in the multilingual classroom, we felt it would be helpful to include here examples of how teachers have set abour acquiring some knowledge of pupils' languages and how they and their pupils have benefited as a result.

Making a start

If you are not in the habit of encouraging your pupils to share their languages and cultures with you, you will want to find a starting point that lends itself naturally to discussion. A teacher of younger juniors approached this through cookery activities. The children taking part were all Bengali speakers and she suggested they choose a dish with which they were familiar:

> *After some discussion the children decided they would like to make chapattis and a potato curry . . . they made the dough for the chapattis and left it on the side in bowls while they prepared their vegetables — tomatoes, onions and potatoes. As they were working they talked together in their mother tongue . . . In English we discussed the herbs they were going to use and they taught me the Bengali names for them . . .*

The children went on to prepare the meal following the procedures with which they were familiar from home. They gave their teacher a running commentary and wherever appropriate introduced the Bengali words for the ingredients and utensils. The success of this activity lay in the fact that the children were on familiar ground; they were able to take the lead, using skills and displaying knowledge which they had acquired at home. So discussion about the Bengali names for different foodstufffs and cooking equipment arose without a great deal of prompting from the teacher.

A teacher of rising-fives found her starting point quite by chance:

> *I was sewing with a group of children when one of the boys asked me to pass him the 'canchee'. I did not respond immediately and*

the child realised that I did not understand, so he repeated to me 'the scissors please'. From this the child and his friend enjoyed telling me the names for needle, material, cotton, etc. in Panjabi.

For several weeks previous to this I had made various attempts at discovering the Panjabi words for different things related to topic work and classroom objects but with no great success. The children were not unwilling to help but it was a rather laboured activity and I did not want to impose a false situation on them. From this incident however the children have been able and willing to teach me various words and phrases in Panjabi as and when the situation arises.

Her conclusion aptly sums up the experience of other teachers:

This has reinforced my belief that children are willing to help when the situation has a real meaning and value to them and when the classroom atmosphere has been well established to support their bilingualism.

Beyond these initial steps in the classroom some teachers have tried to be more systematic about extending their knowledge of vocabulary and phrases:

. . . I began learning Panjabi with the aid of a couple of parents and several children. I began by asking them to translate individual words and simple phrases which I then wrote down in a phonetic form. I soon found it useful to compile a simple dictionary with the words arranged under certain headings, e.g., food, clothes, school, etc. and with an index so that I could refer to and classify new material easily.

An element of self-help features also in the following example from a group of teachers who collaborated with bilingual colleagues to prepare a list of simple expressions which they considered would be useful for teachers working in the early years of the primary school. The list was kept simple so that they could learn it quickly and easily. The expressions were divided into sections and phonetically transliterated into Urdu. An accompanying tape was made. Examples of the kind of words and phrases included are given in the chart opposite. Note that the commands are only suitable for addressing children.

Of course, the example quoted is from an area of the country where a particular community language is especially prevalent. In other areas of the country the linguistic situation is by no means so clearly defined. Schools may contain a wide range of languages and teachers may consequently have difficulty deciding which, if any, to pursue. But, even in

It is impossible to present the Urdu/Hindi words in English transcription without some explanation of the sounds this represents. Sounds occurring in the list below are pronounced approximately as follows. They are listed in the order in which they occur.

a – as in *about*
ā – as in *father*
ai – like the *a* in *hand*
u – as in *put*
e – as in the *ay* of *may*
i – as in *machine*
t and d are dental – made with the tongue touching the teeth.
ṭ and ṛ are retroflex – made with the tip of the tongue turned back.
c – like English *ch* in *church*
h – following a consonant indicates that outgoing breath must be heard as you say it. These 'aspirated' sounds sound quite different to South Asian ears from the 'unaspirated' ones.
ṅ – indicates that the preceding vowel is nasalised.
au – rather like English *o* in *not*
kh – is like the *ch* in Scottish *loch*

GREETINGS

The only universally acceptable greetings etc. are *Hello* and *Goodbye*. The BBC TV programmes for Asians use them. All others are specific to particular religions. The first two on the following list are only used between Muslims.

For Hindus, both the greeting and the response is *namaste* or *namaskar*

For Sikhs, both the greeting and the response is *sat srī akāl*.

GREETINGS	RESPONSE
Peace be with you *as salām alaikum*	and also with you *vālaikum as salām*
What is your name? *tumhārā nām kyā hai?*	my name is *merā nām . . . hai.*

INSTRUCTIONS

everybody *sab*	come here *idhar āo*
stop *ruk jāo*	sit down *baiṭho/baiṭh jāo*
look at me *muje dekho*	everybody sit down *sab baiṭho/sab baiṭh jāo*
listen *suno*	make a line *lāin banao*

WORDS FOR MATHS

nothing *kuch nahīṅ*	one *ek*	six *chai*
	two *do*	seven *sāt*
	three *tīn*	eight *āṭh*
	four *cār*	nine *nau*
	five *pāṅc*	ten *das*
big *baṛā, -e, -í* *		little *chotā, -e, -ī* *

COLOURS

red *lál/surkh*	green *harā, -e, -i* * *sabz*
blue *nīlā, -e, -ī* *	purple *udā, -e, -ī* *
brown *bhūrā, -e, -ī* *	black *kālā, -e, -ī* */ *syāh*
yellow *pīlā, -e, -i* * *zard*	white *safed*

* these endings vary according to the noun qualified

-a for masculine singular nouns
-e for masculine plural
-i for feminine nouns whether singular or plural.

these circumstances, the list of vocabulary and expressions we have quoted is sufficiently concise to provide a possible framework for helping teachers obtain a smattering of several of the languages used in their classrooms.

Benefits for teachers and children

We have stressed already that learning another language to a level where you can communicate effectively with others is a long, complex and often frustrating process, and the strategies we have outlined so far are really just a small beginning. Nevertheless, teachers who have tried some of these approaches have found that they can be of benefit in several ways. With this in mind we set out below, in teachers' own words, some of the benefits they have described:

Learning and using your pupils' languages — some benefits

"I am now more aware of how much strain we can be putting on our pupils when we expect them to spend all day learning through their second language."

"Some of the children who had been reluctant to talk in their mother tongues began to be much less embarrassed about doing so."

"It has helped all the children to realise that all their languages are valued in the classroom."

"I now realise how difficult it can be to learn a new language that is totally alien to my own."

"I think the fact that a teacher is trying to learn their language has given status to the children."

"Parents are pleased that I am making the effort . . . a father came in to say he did not want his children to lose touch with their home language."

"The children enjoy taking the role of teacher and I feel this has strengthened our relationship."

"Parents are now far more confident about coming in to school to discuss matters regarding their children and to offer their help to us."

Learning in depth

Other teachers, who have found themselves developing a strong interest in their pupils' languages, have decided to pursue one or more of them in depth through a course of instruction[1]. There follows an account of how one teacher has approached this and, particularly, the uses she has made of her knowledge in her day-to-day work with children.

Most of the children I teach have been Panjabi-speaking Sikhs or Muslims; some of these have been very young children — nursery or rising-fives — who have had virtually no English. Occasionally, I have taught older children who have just come to England and have had no English. I felt that some knowledge of the children's mother tongue would be very useful in these early stages; and fortunately I have been able to attend Panjabi classes, along with several other teachers and other interested parties — including a vicar, a policeman, and a postwoman.

We have enjoyed our Panjabi lessons a lot; each week, as we've learnt a new construction or some new words, new light has dawned on us. For instance, many an infant teacher has wondered why all Panjabi-speaking children seem to call their cats 'Billy'. The explanation is that 'billi' is the Panjabi word for 'cat'. Similarly, when we are naming parts of the body and I point to my nose, and a child says 'nak', I now know that she is correctly saying 'nose' in Panjabi, and not incorrectly saying 'neck'.

One teacher was full of remorse for having delivered a severe dressing-down to a child who had muttered, as she thought, 'crab'! 'How dare you call me a crab, you rude boy?' This child had, in fact, made a mistake in his writing, and was muttering 'kraab' — that is, 'horrible' — about his work.

Sometimes now, if I know the Panjabi word, I use it in my teaching of English. One day, I had collected my group of 'beginners' from the rising-fives and the reception class, and we were walking through the reception area of the school, where there are books and soft toys. One of these was a small lion, and Ishtiaq remarked to his friends as he picked it up, 'billi'. 'No', I said, 'It's not a billi — it's a lion.' The Panjabi for 'lion' having quite forsaken me, I uttered a loud roar, to the astonishment of the Head and several visitors who were also passing. 'Ah', said Ishtiaq, 'Sheer'. 'Yes', I said. 'Sheer — lion!'.

This is only a small point; but without my smattering of Panjabi, I would have missed both Ishtiaq's initial confusion, and the opportunity of clearing it up. I also find I understand some of the children's difficulties with English much better; for instance, 'his' and 'her' cause a good deal of confusion. This is because, to take an example, the Panjabi word for 'book' is 'kitaab', and is feminine. So, 'Oh dee kitaab' means both 'his book' and 'her book'. The Panjabi word for 'dog' is 'kutaa' and is masculine. So, 'Oh daa kataa' means 'his dog' and 'her dog'. We have all learnt a genuine respect for our pupils' bilingualism, humbly reflecting on how much better their 'beginners' English is than our beginners' Panjabi.

Putting skills to use

With our final example we show how some teachers have managed to achieve an impressive level of competence in their pupils' languages. This account comes from just such a teacher, whose knowledge of Gujarati enables her to work with bilingual helpers to teach mother tongue rhymes to her pupils and prepare simple bilingual reading material based on the children's accounts of their own experiences.

For some time I have felt the need for simple reading material which was relevant to the child and which used familiar names and situations. With this in mind I hit upon the idea of producing a series of small reading books based on incidents which had happened to the children at school or at home. For example, Fahida frightening a teacher with a toy spider, or Salim losing his car.

First, the stories were written and illustrated by the children. We translated them into Gujarati and then went on to print them as bilingual books with a transliteration to enable monolingual teachers and children to use them. The length of the books (4 to 10 sentences) and the simple construction made this possible.

When we first came to put the books into use we met with the inevitable giggles. But the children soon accepted them and seemed to appreciate our genuine efforts to communicate using the mother tongue.

We are also teaching Gujarati rhymes, with actions, assisted by bilingual adults. These have appealed to all the children irrespective of their home language. All teachers now have copies in Gujarati, a transliteration and a translation of the rhyme into English. So the teacher can use it as part of his/her classroom work.

She concludes:

It is difficult to convey in words the warm atmosphere that develops in a class where the children feel that everything they can offer is appreciated, and the pleasure of the parents when they hear what we are trying to do. I have noticed that children who appear very withdrawn in class often blossom and talk exuberantly during a story in Gujarati, where they are using the language which comes most easily to them.

I have been amazed at the level of understanding that 6–7-year-olds show in explaining features of Gujarati to me. All I can say to the sceptical teacher is, take the first step, introduce the mother tongue in this small way and enjoy the experience with your children.

74

me ek bilaa Dee paaLee chhe	I have a pet, it's a cat
te range bahu rapaaLee chhe	My cat is beautiful
te Halve, haLve Chaale chhe	She walks slowly slowly
ne andaaraama bhaaLe chhe	She can see, even in the dark
daheen khay, doodh khay	She eats yogurt and drinks milk
ghee to chap chap chaatee jaay	And likes to eat ghee
te underne jatpat jaale	She catches mice very quickly
pan kuutraathee beetee chaale	But is scared of dogs
enaa Dil par Dagh chhe	She has got stripes on her body
e maaraa gharno vagh chhe	As if she is the tiger of my house.

ABC tapelaa maa ghee	ABC There's ghee in the pan
ghee vari rotli	The chapatti is buttered
Fazila ni chotli	Like Fazila's plait

6 Looking at resources

> *I find that I have to be very inventive and resourceful when collecting materials for supporting language diversity. There's quite a lot available but it has to be searched for . . . sometimes in the most unlikely places.*

As this statement suggests, compiling suitable resources is probably one of the more pressing priorities facing teachers who wish to give recognition to their pupils' language experiences. Like other new aspects of the curriculum there is no ready-made solution. In these circumstances, teachers are falling back on a variety of well-established approaches like turning for advice and assistance to:

* local Library and Museum Services;
* Teachers' Centres;
* Language Centres and Multicultural Support Services;
* LEA advisers for Multicultural Education, English as a second language, and Modern Languages;
* Development Education agencies;
* commercial publishers and manufacturers of educational materials;
* firms or public services (e.g., Health Education Council) that produce free materials for educational purposes.

Teachers are also using their professional ingenuity to prepare their own materials for meeting specific classroom needs or to compensate for deficiencies in existing commercially available resources. This often leads to them calling upon the expertise of bilingual colleagues and members of the school's non-teaching staff, as well as parents and others from the local community. Indeed, the community itself, in the form of local shops, community centres, places of worship and entertainment, will sometimes be seen as a resource to be tapped.

Some approaches

In this final chapter we look at some of the ways in which you might go about compiling resources for the multilingual classroom by:

* finding out more about materials already published in community languages;
* using other resources that may be available in the classroom;
* adapting resources originally prepared for helping with English language development;
* developing materials of your own.

The chapter is not intended as a definitive guide to resources. Its purpose is to outline some of the approaches that are currently being taken in schools and thus offer you guidance as you set about extending your own classroom resources in order to support a curriculum that reflects more fully your pupils' languages.

Existing materials

We begin by looking at materials, already published in the mother tongue, from overseas sources as well as here in Britain.

Most of the community language materials available to schools have been printed and published overseas. Some primary teachers have tended to dismiss these on the grounds that they are often poorly printed on inferior paper, with bindings that are not sufficiently robust for classroom use and content which reflects a world beyond the experience of bilingual children growing up in urban multicultural Britain. Underlying such criticisms has been a feeling that if children's mother tongues are to be given equal status with English then the materials used should be of comparable quality with those normally on offer in the primary classroom.

We share this view about the status of materials but as we look around we are finding increasingly that there is no longer such a wide disparity. Primary teachers have always used a variety of materials, ranging from hard-cover textbooks to cheaply produced consumable workbooks, and including paperback stories, alphabet charts, board games and posters. A similar range is now available in many of the languages spoken by ethnic minority children. Of course, we are not suggesting that these exist on anything like the same scale as commercially produced English materials nor that the quality is consistently comparable, but the point we wish to stress is that the situation is far more encouraging than you may previously have assumed.

We are encouraged by the variety of materials we have seen in use in classrooms and on display at LEA Multicultural Resource Centres. These included alphabet charts, games for picture-word recognition, colouring books of traditional patterns, folk-tales and simple reading material, all of which can be bought through ethnic minority distributors and community bookshops. As you begin to give more consideration to materials like these which cannot be obtained through your normal channels, you will probably find yourself asking a number of questions, especially:

* how can I find out what is available in particular languages; and
* if I do not speak the languages myself, how can I be sure that the materials are suitable?

Most towns and cities now have community bookshops serving minority interests which are not catered for by the major booksellers[1]. Often they will carry small stocks of community language materials and will give you every assistance in obtaining a varied selection for classroom use. You should therefore try to make contact with any shops of this sort in your own area and see just what type of service they are able to offer. Other local, yet little used, sources of materials are ethnic minority newsagents. Apart from carrying the normal newsagent's range these will sometimes have a variety of reading matter, including books and comics for children in the main languages of the local community. Again, you should make a point of finding out where your local shops are and building up contact with them. We have met many teachers who have been pleasantly surprised at finding such convenient 'resource centres'.

Without doubt, however, your main source of classroom materials will be the larger ethnic minority book distributors, many of whom are based in the London area[2]. Most of these now supply their own catalogues which detail the materials they can offer for particular languages. sometimes with guidance on age or interest levels. Unfortunately, no catalogue can be a substitute for seeing materials, especially books, at first hand. We would therefore suggest that you try to visit some of the shops yourself, preferably by prior arrangement, giving some advance information on your areas of interest (age group, subject matter, languages, and so on). Teachers who have done this have often been very impressed with the quality of the advice they have received.

This latter point may go some way towards helping you over the problem of selecting materials in languages which you do not understand. Certainly it may help ensure that the reading and interest levels are appropriate for your pupils. But, as we stressed earlier, selecting materials also entails thinking about questions of style, register, appeal of visuals, cultural appropriateness and bias in terms of gender or race. To do this effectively you will need to call upon the expertise of others such as bilingual colleagues or friends, parents or members of your local community.

Locally produced materials

Teachers' Centres, Languages Centres and Multicultural Support Services have long been associated with the development of materials to meet specific local needs. Sometimes these have come about in order to compensate for deficiencies in the materials available through commercial publishers. In other cases they have set out to extend particular sets of resources that were originally produced by publishers. And many have simply been prepared by local groups of teachers, and the centre has offered facilities for printing and distribution.

The quality of these locally-originated materials will vary according to the expertise and facilities available but their importance lies in the fact that they have appeared as a result of teachers seeing an area of need that was not being adequately catered for by existing resources, and setting out to do something about it.

In view of this self-help tradition, it is not surprising to find that several centres are now actively involved in developing resources for supporting some of the various languages of their local communities.

There are now a range of materials that have originated in this way. Most of them are story books, for use in the classroom, produced in one particular language and possibly including a parallel English text. A number of posters, showing different sorts of greetings, have also been produced and some centres are now beginning to prepare cassette versions of well-known stories.

It is not possible to provide a detailed guide to the community language materials developed in different areas of the country but in the reference section at the end of the book, we list the names and addresses of centres that have been active in the field[3]. If you are not yet in touch with them you may wish to make contact in order to find out more about the publications they have available. Generally, centres like these are very happy to respond to requests from outside their areas but there are some points that you should bear in mind:

* They are not commercial publishers and therefore do not have staff whose sole function is to deal with orders or requests for information. Often this work is done by people who have many other duties in the centre as well as responsibilities to their local schools. You should therefore try to be specific about the information you want (which languages, age group, etc.). And when ordering materials you should ensure that payment, address details, etc. are correct so as to avoid unnecessary additional work for the centre.
* The materials are not intended to compete with whatever commercial publishers may have available. They are essentially local materials, cheaply produced for local needs.
* The people responsible for the materials will have gone to considerable lengths to ensure that they are of good standard and that close attention has been paid to the quality of the calligraphy and the suitability of the text. But if you have any comments in these areas we are sure they would be well received.
* Finally, any other feedback, particularly on how you have made use of the materials and the responses of children, would be helpful to the centre when they come to carry out revisions or produce notes of guidance for teachers.

Materials from publishers

When making decisions about what to publish, educational publishers will wish to balance commercial considerations against what they know to be educationally sound and desirable. As a result new types of material will usually be made available only when there is sufficient evidence of demand among teachers to ensure a worthwhile commercial return. This has certainly been the case with classroom materials of a multicultural nature. For some years publishers' representatives maintained that since these were of minority appeal it would be difficult to make out a commercial case for them. But as the arguments for a multicultural curriculum for all children gained ground so publishers began to acknowledge that they could make a contribution. Similar issues have come to the fore as publishers have begun to consider their role in relation to materials in the languages of ethnic minority communities. Without doubt, many would now accept the educational case for such materials being made available at a standard comparable with other classroom resources, but difficulties arise over the size and viability of the audiences. Quite simply, publishers need to know whether there will be sufficient take-up from teachers to justify their financial outlay. Not surprisingly, it is only very recently that teachers have been able to see community language materials becoming available, and even then only on a limited basis. The materials that are now available tend to fall into four main categories:

* Those that have been imported to Britain from countries where there is more of a tradition of publishing in ethnic minority languages. The *City Kids* books (published by Nelson) are an example, having originally appeared in Australia where there is substantial state funding for mother tongue teaching programmes.
* Titles that have proved successful, in English, in multicultural classrooms and whose applications might be further extended through being made available in a bilingual format. The Ezra Jack Keats books, *Peter's Chair* and *Whistle for Willie* (Bodley Head), are examples.
* A variation on this theme is for the publisher to produce captions, in community languages, for sticking underneath the English text of a story, thus providing a bilingual edition at minimum cost. Here the *Terraced House* (Methuen) series provides a model which other publishers might emulate. However, with this approach there are two important points to bear in mind. First, themes that may be acceptable in English may not be directly transferable into other languages. For example, stories featuring pork-based meats would be sure to give offence if translated into Urdu for use with Muslim children. Secondly, although we admire the underlying resourcefulness, we would want to stress that publishers, or indeed anybody else taking up the idea, should pay close attention to the quality of the translation and the calligraphy, either of which could mar an otherwise laudable initiative.
* As yet there are few examples of mother tongue materials that have been specifically designed by publishers for use in the British context. Among the few are the *World in a City* packs (ILEA Learning Materials Service/Commission for Racial Equality) which, though intended for use with secondary-age pupils, could have some applications with older juniors who are literate in their mother tongues and who might therefore benefit from being able to follow some of the curriculum in this way.

Despite these several initiatives, however, it is clear that publishing in community languages in Britain is still in is early stages, and although some publishers are sufficiently convinced of the merits of the case to give this area more priority in future, many continue to remain sceptical. What is needed, then, is for teachers to make their needs known through offering suggestions, possibly following some of the ideas already mentioned, as to how more publishers might join those who have already made a start.

Using other resources

So far our discussion has been limited to those materials that are available from published sources. But teachers have pointed out that there are many other resources which, though not originally conceived as aids to children using their mother tongues and learning about linguistic diversity, can nevertheless be extremely useful in giving recognition to children's languages and creating a classroom atmosphere where children feel at ease when using the mother tongue. Resources available from local shops include greetings cards for Chinese New Year, Diwali and Eid, calendars and comics. To these we could add posters, advertising materials, printed carrier bags and food packaging, all of which can help bring a multilingual flavour to classroom displays whilst also providing useful resource material for topic work on linguistic diversity.

If you have not yet made use of materials like these we would suggest that you make contact with the shops near your school where for a small outlay you would probably be able to obtain a varied and useful selection which could be added to your personal, or school, resource bank. For the benefit of other colleagues you could compile a list of appropriate shops in the neighbourhood and the materials that they have to offer.

Adapting materials

To complement materials that are already available in your pupils' languages you might like to consider how you can use or adapt classroom resources which were originally introduced for supporting children's English language development. This has the obvious economic attraction of making the maximum possible use of available resources. More importantly, though, by providing continuity between the materials used for mother tongue support and those associated with mainstream learning, you would be helping to enhance the status of community languages among all children in the class.

Translating storybooks

A starting point could be to translate some of the more popular classroom storybooks and, with the help of gummed labels, produce either bilingual or monolingual mother tongue versions. An example we mentioned earlier is the production by the publishers, Methuen, of Bengali and Urdu versions of the Terraced House readers[4].

If you are thinking of trying this approach there are some points that should be borne in mind:

* permission should be obtained from publishers before producing translated versions of published materials;
* once permission has been obtained publishers will like to be kept informed of developments with a view to assessing the potential market for such ideas;
* there are advantages and disadvantages to both monolingual and bilingual texts; these need to be considered in relation to the needs of the children and the uses to which the materials will be put;
* there should be careful liaison between yourself and the translator in order to produce a text appropriate to the age, ability and interest levels of the children;
* if the translations are to be handwritten careful attention should be paid to the size, clarity and correctness of the script.

Using other resources

Apart from translating reading materials into the mother tongue, you could also consider how other existing resources might be adapted for encouraging mother tongue use or raising awareness of language diversity.

A starting point would be to identify which materials already available in the classroom are of proven value for conceptual and language development in English. You could then examine ways in which these could be used in a multilingual context.

Teachers who have adopted this approach have often been surprised at the versatility of normal classroom materials. One teacher of nursery-age children, for instance, was able to involve bilingual parents in extending the applications of the LDA Sound Lotto[5] pack.

From this experience the same teacher has now gone on to explore the scope of other classroom materials such as games, mathematical apparatus, sand and water equipment, cooking utensils, constructional toys, art and craft media and domestic artefacts. She has found that all of these can be exploited in such a way as to encourage children to interact comfortably through the mother tongue and demonstrate their language skills.

She points out, though, that some of the more widely-used commercial materials contain illustrations that are very specific to a white, indigenous, middle-class culture. These, she suggests, are beyond the experience of many children and can present difficulties to young bilingual children whose cultural perceptions affect their interpretation of visual symbols.

It is important, therefore, that you should bear in mind a number of criteria. We present these in the form of questions which you could use as a simple checklist for selecting materials:

* To what extent do the materials reflect the children's environments and home cultures?
* Are they likely to encourage the children to discuss their experiences at home and in the community?
* To what degree do they show a multicultural or world view?

* Do they lend themselves to topic activities?
* Can they be used by the whole class or are they specific to bilingual children?
* Do they display any cultural or gender bias?

Developing new materials

Primary teachers are well-accustomed to devising materials for classroom use, particularly to meet specific needs that are not adequately catered for by commercial sources. So it is not surprising that many are now applying their ingenuity to developing materials that reflect their pupils' diverse language backgrounds. Charts about the weather, days of the week, colours and letters; games for matching, lotto and snap; number strips, signs and labels; translations of familiar songs, these are some of the many areas in which teachers are devising multilingual materials.

Typical of the approaches being followed is the work of a group of teachers in an authority where Gujarati, Panjabi and Urdu are the main community languages. With a number of bilingual colleagues they have held occasional workshops where they have prepared games, signs, songs and other resources that feature their local languages.

This final section of the book chiefly draws examples from the work of these teachers and from their experiences of using their locally-developed materials.

Like many teachers elsewhere, their starting point was a realisation that although they had *never actually discouraged children from using their mother tongues*, there was a great deal more they could be doing actively *to encourage and stimulate children to display their abilities in languages other than English* and to help *all children become more aware of other languages*. Their workshops with bilingual colleagues provided opportunities for preparing resources that could help remedy the situation.

One teacher concentrated upon number games and friezes which she later displayed in the classroom.

Music and singing were also found to be good ways of opening up use of the mother tongue, particularly when teachers themselves were prepared to learn some words of languages represented in their class:

I introduced the song 'Heads and Shoulders' *and sang it in English to the children. After this I sang the same song in Panjabi. Several children's eyes lit up. They told me that what I was singing was correct Panjabi. The children were asked if they would like to learn the song in Panjabi and without exception they wholeheartedly agreed. Gradually the song was learned by the class. We recorded our efforts on tape . . . This lesson was a great success and provided an excellent starting point for some work on* 'Ourselves'.

In the case of this teacher the work about 'Ourselves' later developed into a large-scale project involving the whole class. We include an extract from the account of the project as an example of how, from such a small beginning, a teacher can begin to change the atmosphere of his/her classroom and, in the process, extend his/her own awareness of children's language experiences.

Two groups have recently recorded information about themselves on tape in Gujarati, Urdu, Pushtu and Bengali, and were not self-conscious about speaking in their mother tongue in front of me. I particularly liked the way in which these groups worked so well together. If any child was not sure of the Urdu or Gujarati word the other children would help him or her out. If a word wasn't pronounced correctly by a child the others corrected him/her. The atmosphere in the class was great . . . I envisage further work on this project of 'Ourselves' leading to booklets in English/Urdu, English/Gujarati and English/Bengali to accompany the tape recordings already made. I would then like to develop a topic on food using a similar approach. I hope to get some parents to come to school to demonstrate and talk about the various aspects of cookery.

In fact all the teachers in the group consistently found that once they had allowed language diversity onto the agenda of the classroom, they were able to elicit responses from bilingual pupils that previously had not been possible. They also began to appreciate the importance of reviewing their own classroom techniques, particularly the value of placing themselves 'in a learning position', enabling the pupils to assume a teaching role.
A number of general points have emerged from the experiences of these and other teachers:

* Children are likely to be more confident and relaxed using their mother tongue if it is seen to be part of a familiar classroom activity rather than a completely new idea which the teacher has introduced solely for the purpose of encouraging mother tongue use.
* Many bilingual materials can be developed for use during normal classroom teaching; these offer much scope for pupil-pupil interaction. Such materials could be incorporated into existing mainstream resources. They could be included, for example, in curriculum development packs available at Teachers' Centres.
* Many teachers find that offering some vocabulary in the mother tongue through topic work is a good starting point for establishing a multilingual atmosphere in the classroom.
* The example of a group of teachers from different schools meeting together to pool experience and to work with bilingual colleagues proved to be a particularly helpful exercise, not only in terms of producing materials but as an in-service experience. Many individual teachers are developing their own approaches to teaching multilingual classes, and it is important that opportunities are provided for these initiatives to be coordinated and experience disseminated.

Conclusion

How can we find out more about the languages of our bilingual pupils? How can we recognise these in a way that will help all children become more aware of the languages of others? How can parents and local communities give their support to the work of the multilingual classroom?

In all our discussions with primary teachers these are the sort of questions that have been raised most frequently. It is significant that they are all concerned with the 'how' rather than the 'why', as this seems to be the stage that many teachers have reached. They accept the educational case for supporting their pupils' mother tongues and now want advice on how they might set about it. That was the starting point for this book.

But we have found that as teachers become involved with the approaches we have described, other more wide-reaching questions begin to emerge for them. How can we acknowledge the dialects of English that are also a part of the multilingual classroom? What changes are needed in teaching styles if children are to have more opportunity to learn from each other, and if we are to be able to learn from our pupils? And how does learning about linguistic diversity fit into our overall strategy for counteracting racist feelings among children?

Whilst we would like to think that the book has something to say about these issues, we are very aware that they are only now coming to the fore among teachers. There is no doubt, however, that they highlight major lines of development for the future and in so doing offer important challenges to us all as we think about the continuing needs of children growing up in a multilingual society.

References and further reading

1   The Schools Council Mother Tongue Project ran between May 1981 and August 1985 with funding provided jointly by the Schools Council and the European Commission. It was concerned with preparing resources for use by bilingual teachers in developing the mother tongue skills of primary age children, and in giving guidance to non-bilingual teachers on how they can provide for linguistic diversity as part of their normal classroom work in the primary school. For further information contact: The Information Section, School Curriculum Development Committee, Newcombe House, 45 Notting Hill Gate, London W11 3JB. Materials produced by the Project are available from Philip and Tacey Ltd, North Way, Andover, Hants, SP10 5BA.

2   *Supporting Children's Bilingualism* – policy issues for schools and LEAs, by David Houlton and Richard Willey, available from Longman Resources Unit, 33–35 Tanner Row, York, YO1 1JP. Price £2.00.

Introduction
1   For a more detailed discussion about research into bilingualism among children and the benefits of mother tongue teaching:
Bilingualism in Education by John Wright, published by ISSUES, 11 Carleton Gardens, Brecknock Road, London N15 5AQ
Mother Tongue – Politics and Practice, published by ISSUES, *see above*.
Many Voices – Bilingualism, Culture and Education by Jane Miller, published by Routledge and Kegan Paul

Finding out about children's languages
1   This quote is from an article by John Rose in *Time Out* (11.7.80).
2   A valuable discussion about the wider linguistic context in which children operate outside school can be found in the report of the Linguistic Minorities Project – *Linguistic Minorities in England* available from Tinga, Tinga Ltd., Darby House, Bletchingley Road, Merstham, Redhill, Surrey. Price £2.95, plus 50p postage.
3   A useful introduction to dialect in education is contained in Peter Trudgill's *Accent, Dialect and the School*, published by Edward Arnold. You will also find it helpful to read *Language in Multicultural Classrooms* by Viv Edwards, published by Batsford.
4   A more detailed example of a questionnaire designed for use by pupils in school is the Linguistic Minorities Project's *Secondary Pupils Survey*. Further information from: The Information Office, University of London Institute of Education, 20 Bedford Way, London WC1H 0AL.
5   This is a point that has been made by other writers who have worked with teachers in order to investigate children's linguistic ranges. For instance, *Languages and Dialects of London School Children* by Harold Rosen and Tony Burgess, published by Ward Lock Educational.
6   *Languages of the World* by Kenneth Katzner, published by Routledge and Kegan Paul. Other useful sources of information are the *Language* and *Culture* guides produced by CILT (see p. 88).
7   The idea referred to here is taken from the *Children's Language Project* which was produced jointly by the Schools Council Mother Tongue Project and the LINC project and published by Philip and Tacey.

Language diversity across the curriculum
1   The *Children's Language Project* (see note 7 above) contains many suggestions on how linguistic diversity might be incorporated into normal class topic work.
2   One of the most useful sources of ideas for teachers working in this area is the *Languages Book*, which is available from the ILEA English Centre, Sutherland Street, London SW1.
3   There is now a wide variety of recipe books, suitable for primary school use, which draw from different cultures. Your local Teachers Centre or Multicultural Resource Centre will probably be able to offer suggestions. A title that you might find helpful is *Recipes from around the world* published by Oxfam Education Dept, and available from 274 Banbury Road, Oxford OX2 7DZ, price £2.95.
4   We have already mentioned that dialect issues are covered in some detail in Viv Edwards's *Language in Multicultural Classrooms*. The same

book also has, in its resources section, some suggestions for additional reading on the subject as well as some publications that may be of value as classroom resources. Ideas for looking specifically at Black English are also well covered in the book, but suggestions of a more practical nature can be found in Steve Hoyle's series of articles in the Commission for Racial Equality *Education Journal* (Vol 3 No.3 and Vol 4 No. 1).

5   See for example the articles by Audrey Gregory and Norah Woollard in *Child Education* (July 1982). A useful resource pack for primary teachers is *All Children Play – background information on play in multi-racial Britain*. This is published by Fair Play for Children and available from them at 248 Kentish Town Road, London NW5, price £2.50.

Working with others in school and community

1   For a more detailed treatment of some of these issues see: *Home and School in Multicultural Britain* by Sally Tomlinson, published by Batsford (1984).

2   A number of LEAs and schools have now begun to develop booklets and other resources in community languages in order to introduce ethnic minority parents to aspects of school life. See, the Bradford LEA's *Starting School* and the publications produced by the Coventry LEA.

3   One of the first attempts to document the provision that ethnic minority communities themselves make for language maintenance was Verity S. Khan's *Provision by minorities for language maintenance* (in *Bilingualism and British Education – the dimensions of diversity*, published by the Centre for Information on Language Teaching and Research). This is a useful introduction to the range of community provision and the reasons underlying it.

4   For a fuller discussion of strategies for building closer links with community mother tongue classes see *Supporting Children's Bilingualism* by David Houlton and Richard Willey (see p. 00, note 2).

Collecting and using mother tongue stories

1   Books published by the Children's Book Trust of New Delhi are available in Britain through many community bookshops (see p. 89).

2   THE MICE AND THE ELEPHANT was broadcast by BBC Schools Radio as part of its MOTHER TONGUE SONG AND STORY series. The languages included in the series were: Cypriot Greek, Cypriot Turkish, Bengali, Sylheti Bengali, Panjabi, Mirpuri Panjabi, Gujarati and Cantonese. An illustrated booklet to accompany the series is available (price £1.25 incl p&p) from: Mother Tongue Song and Story, Multicultural Curriculum Support Service, Educational Development Centre, 36 Wolverhampton Road, Walsall, West Midlands, WS2 8PN.

3   See, for example, Gillian Klein's *Resources for Multicultural Education – an introduction*, published by Longman Resources Unit (address above). You will also find it helpful to consult *Finding Out About Children's Books* which is a booklet produced by the Open University as part of its 'Children, Language and Literature' course for serving teachers.

4   Advice on extending storytelling in order to support learning in other areas of the curriculum is contained in the Teachers Notes accompanying

the video material produced by the ILEA *Second Language in the Primary School Project*. Information on this is available from the ILEA Learning Materials Service, 275 Kennington Lane, London SE11 5QZ.

5   *Rupa the Elephant* is published by the Children's Book Trust of New Delhi, many of whose publications are available from the booksellers listed on p. 89.

6   *The Banyan Tree* is one of a series of books produced in community languages by the Newham LEA's Centre for Multicultural Education, New City Road, London E13.

Learning and using your pupils' languages

1   Teachers wanting information on opportunities for learning community languages will find it helpful to consult the *Language and Culture Guides*, published by the Centre for Information on Language Teaching and Research, 20 Carlton House Terrace, London SW1. These include details on the range of courses available for particular languages. For private study, look at Ralph Russell's *A New Course in Hindustani for Learners in Britain*. This is one of the few published schemes suitable for adult learners of community languages, and is used for teaching by the author. Available from the School of Oriental and African Studies, Malet Street, London WC1, the course is in four parts: Part 1 – £3.00, Part 2 – £3.00, Part 3 – £4.00, and Part 4 – £3.00. A C60 cassette is available to accompany Part 1, price £3.45.

Looking at resources

1   A list of some of the main out-of-London community language bookshops is provided on p. 89.

2   Details of some of the main London-based booksellers are on p. 90.

3   Some of the LEA Teachers Centres that have developed materials in community languages are:

Bedfordshire	Resources Centre Acacia Road Bedford MK42 0HV (Tel: 0234–64475)
	Multi-racial Education Resources Centre c/o Denbigh Junior School Denbigh Road Luton LU3 1NS (Tel: 0582–507757)
Coventry	Minority Group Support Service South Street Hillfields Coventry CV1 5EJ (Tel: 0203–26888)
Lancashire	Blackburn Language Centre Accrington Road Blackburn Lancs. BB1 2AS

Leicestershire	ESL Advisory Service
	Rushey Mead Centre
	Harrison Road
	Leicester LE4 7PA (Tel: 0533–680224)
Newham	Centre for ESL
	In-Service Education Centre
	New City School
	New City Road
	Plaistow
	London E13 9PY (Tel: 01–552–5719)
Walsall	Multi-Cultural Education Support Services
	Education Development Centre
	36 Wolverhampton Road
	Walsall
	West Midlands (Tel: 0922–613125)
Waltham Forest	English Language Centre
	Markhouse Road
	London E17 8BD

4   Details of the TERRACED HOUSE series and the titles that are available with community language texts can be obtained from: Methuen Educational, 11 New Fetter Lane, London EC4P 4EE.

5   The LDA SOUND LOTTO PACK is available from: LDA, Duke Street, Wisbech, Cambridgeshire, PE13 2AE.

Booksellers and publishers outside the London area

Jayson & Co., 267A Soho Road, Birmingham. Tel. 021-523-6851.
Gohil, 366 Stratford Road, Birmingham. Tel. 021-772-3844.
Islamic Centre, 179 Anderton Road, Birmingham.
Paigham-E-Islam, 423 Stratford Road, Birmingham. Tel. 021-773-8301/2.
Third World Publications, 152 Stratford Road, Birmingham.
Bangladesh Book Centre, 10 Harlow Road, Lidget Green, Bradford.
Tel. 0274-34559.
Mogul Traders, 5 Elizabeth Street, Bradford. Tel. 0274-729009.
Rolex Trading Co., 6 Hallfield Road, Bradford. Tel. 0274-31908.
International Islami Tablighi Mission, 2 New Street, Slaithwaite,
Huddersfield. Tel. 0484-25117.
Bailey Bros. and Swinton Ltd, Warren House, Folkestone, Kent.
Tel. 0303-56501.
Vak News Agency, 91 Harrison Road, Leicester. Tel. 0533-63902.
The Islamic Foundation, 223 London Road, Leicester. Tel. 0533-700725.
Further information on suppliers and publishers of books, periodicals and other community language materials, in Britain and overseas, is contained in *Public Library Services for a multicultural society*, available free from: The Commission for Racial Equality, 10–12 Allington Street, London SW1E 5EH   Tel. 01-828-7022

Booksellers and publishers in the London area

Bengali, Gujarati, Panjabi, Urdu
ABC Magazine Distributors, 7 The Broadway, Southall, Middx. Tel: 01-574 1319 (Panjabi).
Books from India, 32 Coptic Street, London WC1. Tel: 01-580 1228.
Independent Publishing Co (Soma), 38 Kennington Lane, London SE11, Tel: 01-735 2101 (Bengali, Gujarati, Panjabi, Urdu).
Islamic Book Centre, 202 North Gower Street, London NW1. Tel: 01-388 0710 (Bengali, Gujarati, Urdu).
Muslim Welfare House, 233 Seven Sisters Road, London N4. Tel: 01-272 5170 (Bengali, Gujarati, Panjabi, Urdu).
RNB Enterprises, 70 Queens Road, Walthamstow, London E17. Tel: 01-521 6380 (Urdu).
Ruposhi Bangla Ltd. 220 Tooting High Street, London SW17. Tel: 01-672 7843 (Bengali).
Shakti Bookhouse, 46 High Street, Southall, Middx. Tel: 01-574 1325 (Bengali, Gujarati, Panjabi, Urdu).
Virdee, 26 South Road, Southall, Middx. Tel: 01-571 4870 (Gujarati, Panjabi, Urdu).

Arabic
Al Saqi Books, 26 Westbourne Grove, London W2. Tel: 01-229 8543.
Muslim Bookshop, 233 Seven Sisters Road, London N4. 01-272 05170.

Greek
Hellenic Book Service, 122 Charing Cross Road, London WC2. 01-836 7071.
Kimon, 87 Plender Street, London NW1. Tel: 01-387 8809.
Zeno, 6 Denmark Street, London WC2. Tel: 01-836 2522.

Turkish
Basaran Turk Kitabevi, 117 Green Lanes, London N16. Tel: 01-226 3330.

Japanese
Japanese Publications Centre, 5 Warwick Street, London W1. 01-439 8036.
OCS Bookshop, 9 Newport Place, London WC2. Tel: 01-485 4201.

Chinese
Guanghwa Bookshop, 9 Newport Place, London WC2. Tel: 01-437 3737.
New Era Books, 203 Seven Sisters Road, London N4. Tel: 01-272 5894.
Hong Kong Culture Service, 46 Gerrard Street, London W1. 01-734 5037.

Farsi
Iran Book Centre, 223 Old Brompton Road, London SW5. Tel: 01-370 5337 (Most books in Persian (Farsi) Some in Kurdish, Arabic, Armenian).

Polish
Earls Court Publications Ltd. 129–130 Shepherds Bush Centre, Shepherds Bush Green, London W12. Tel: 01-743 2391.
Orbis Books, 66 Kenway Road, London SW5. Tel: 01-370 2210.

Western European Languages
(Spanish, French, Italian, German, Portuguese)
Grant and Cutler, 11 Buckingham Street, London WC2. Tel: 01-839 3136.